810.9 B873e 1973
Brooks, Van Wyck, 1886-1963
Emerson and others

EMERSON AND OTHERS

Emerson and Others

By

Van Wyck Brooks

OCTAGON BOOKS

A Division of Farrar, Straus and Giroux

New York   1973

Copyright, 1927, by E. P. Dutton & Co., Inc.
Copyright renewed 1955 by Van Wyck Brooks

Reprinted 1973
by special arrangement with E. P. Dutton & Co., Inc., New York

OCTAGON BOOKS
A DIVISION OF FARRAR, STRAUS & GIROUX, INC.
19 Union Square West
New York, N. Y. 10003

Library of Congress Cataloging in Publication Data

Brooks, Van Wyck, 1886-1963.
　　Emerson and others.

　　　　CONTENTS: Emerson: six episodes.—John Butler Yeats.–Randolph Bourne.—The letters of Ambrose Bierce. [etc.]

　　　　1. Emerson, Ralph Waldo, 1803-1882.　2. American literature–Addresses, essays, lectures.　I. Title.

PS1631.B63　1973　　　　　　810'.9　　　　　　73-313
ISBN 0-374-90998-9

Printed in USA by
Thomson-Shore, Inc.
Dexter, Michigan

Contents

EMERSON: SIX EPISODES	1
I. THE TRANSCENDENTAL CLUB	3
II. *The Dial*, CONCORD	25
III. THE REFORMERS	47
IV. AT WORK	64
V. LECTURING	78
VI. IN CONCORD	98
JOHN BUTLER YEATS	107
RANDOLPH BOURNE	121
THE LETTERS OF AMBROSE BIERCE	147
AMOR FATI	159
NOTES ON HERMAN MELVILLE	169
THE NOVELS OF UPTON SINCLAIR	207
THE LITERARY LIFE IN AMERICA	219

Note

SEVERAL of the papers collected in this volume have already appeared in print. Those on Randolph Bourne and The Literary Life in America contain many statements that are certainly less true now than they were when they were written; but I have thought it best to reprint them in their first form.

The episodes from Emerson's life are, the reader will observe, written largely in Emerson's own words. I have gathered these from his Journals and other sources with the idea of presenting as directly as possible his own thoughts and feelings.

EMERSON: SIX EPISODES

EMERSON: SIX EPISODES

I

THE TRANSCENDENTAL CLUB

EMERSON was thirty-one when he settled in Concord. The sun had emerged from the clouds: he had come back from his year in England charged with life and vigor. How many memories were associated with this little town! Personal memories, family memories, national memories. The happiest hours of his childhood—hours of escape from the tasks of a Boston schoolboy—had been passed in these peaceful meadows, redolent of the lives of his forbears.

He married the following year, 1835, Lydia Jackson of Plymouth, and moved into the house on the Cambridge turnpike. It was an ample house indeed, square, plain, white, with a Doric portico—not a Plymouth mansion, no, nor a Concord cottage either, but the sage's golden mean. High ceilings, airy chambers, a garden by the brook for the bulbs and seeds from Plymouth, the tulips and the roses, an orchard and a barn; and a study at the front, on the ground-floor, facing northward, a sanctum for the sage. When the fresh wind blew, Emerson placed an Æolian harp in one of the Western windows; and listening to it, fitfully singing in the breeze, he heard the wild melodies of Wales and Provence ringing through him again. Its notes mingled, on spring and summer days, with the trilling of the birds; for outside, between the windows, stood a balsam fir-tree, and in its branches, when the sun was out, robins and cedar-birds, orioles and goldfinches, warblers and catbirds loved to foregather.

Here in Concord were the men that make republics, Greeks like his brother Charles, Romans like Samuel Hoar. And the old names of the old families, the Bloods, the Willards, the Barretts, were all about him, tenon'd and mortised to the farms his fathers had known six generations before. Everything in Concord sang to him. Gay was the sound of the whetting of the scythe, delicious the scent of strawberries on his hands, and the solid sunshine of the pumpkins. And the breath of the warm south wind that drew him to the top of the ridge along the turnpike, where the mountains shimmered in the distance through the summer haze. And the thistle-balls floating upward, and the droning of the bees in the still spaces of the woods; the blue river in the grass at the foot of the meadow, the water soft as milk when he went for a swim. And the flags and the rushes that bordered the torpid stream, the yellow water-lily, the pickerel-weed with its long stalk crowned with a blue spire.

He was lecturing now—the pulpit was forgotten: lecturing in the country Lyceums, a stringent test for the wares of a man of letters. He had become, in fact, the prophet of the new age. It was not so much his ideas that people received as a certain electric shock that energized their latent power and knowledge. What had been vague in their minds became suddenly clear, doubts were transformed into certainties, half-hearted hopes into vigorous resolutions. An invisible authority had come to their support, the authority of their own unconscious natures. And they felt themselves no longer "pinched in a corner, cowards fleeing before a revolution, but redeemers and benefactors, advancing and advancing on chaos and the dark."

But still his life was very lonely in Concord, and he found nothing so fearsome as too much solitude. There was much to be said for society too, and cities; to be isolated was to be sick, and so far dead. Rightly thought Goethe, that dealing habitually with men and affairs was essential to one's health. For one thing, society educated one's will, which never acquired force in solitude. It was true that if Emerson stayed in the city he seemed to lose all substance and became surface in a world of surfaces; everything was external there, and he thought of his hat and coat, and all his other surfaces, and nothing else. But a periodical raid was another matter. He could do his thinking alone, but he had to go to market to get his facts.

On Saturday, as a rule, Emerson left his study and set out for Boston to see what friends he could muster. Down came the silk hat from the shelf in the closet; then followed three long hours in the stage that passed his door. But the passengers were a foretaste of the wide world, and the stage drove through the slums of the North End. How picturesque were the crowds on the sidewalks, how much more enlivening than the clean-shaved and silk-robed procession on Tremont Street! He knew instantly, as he passed them, whence all the fine pictures had their origin; he felt the painter stirring in him. These unrestrained attitudes and manners recalled to him the force and eloquence of form and the sting of color. No suggestion here of those depressing college anniversaries at Cambridge, those hurrahs among the ghosts, those yellow, bald, toothless meetings in memory of red cheeks, black hair and departed health. They were real crowds, wholesome and heart-warming; they restored one's flagging sense of the infinite wealth of humanity.

Then quick to the pavement!—and off he strode, tall, erect, light-footed and strong of limb, with his long neck and his bright blue eyes peering about, one shoulder slightly higher than the other. Where was he going today? To the Sculpture Gallery, perhaps, at the Athenaeum, for a look at Michaelangelo's Day and Night? To a concert of Ole Bull? (A benign influence, that sorcerer, with a sleep as of Egypt on his lips in the midst of his rapturous music, even for a man without an ear.) Or perhaps to the foreign bookstore and reading-room that Dr. Nathaniel Peabody and his daughter Elizabeth had opened in the front parlor of their house in West Street? (Not to one of those literary clubs, be sure, where they still discussed the question, *Who wrote Junius?*) An embarrassment of riches! One trod rather proudly the streets of a town like Boston: Vasari himself never felt more stimulus in the air of his darling Florence. These pavements too had a history: no accident, Boston, no mere cross-roads, tavern or army-barracks, grown up by time and luck to a place of wealth, but a seat of men of principle. How natural that the desire for glory and honor should spring out of it!—so that all who possessed talent were impelled to struggle, and labor by every means to be foremost.

To the Sculpture Gallery, then; Margaret Fuller would be waiting for him there, under that sunny roof, in those airy chambers. There were the casts, selected by Canova, the Laocoön, the Discobolus, the head of the Phidian Zeus, and so many others—Greece and Italy brought bodily to Boston. And there was the Brimmer donation of French and Italian drawings, prints of the Sistine frescoes, prints of Correggio, drawings of Guercino, one apple from every tree. And pictures ascribed to Rembrandt, Poussin, Rubens, painted by God knows whom, obscure, nameless persons, yet with such skill and mastery as to bring connoisseurs in doubt. What color!—a tonic that made him brisk and gay. Rome rose again in his memory, and Paris danced before him. (But how wronged they were, these paintings, discrowned and disgraced, by being crowded together in one apartment!—

like so many men lowered by juxtaposition. One picture at a time! Let the eye conspire with the painter, carry his work out far and wide, see more than he has done, see what he meant to do, enjoy the unity of the hour!)

A glowing companion, Margaret, in these adventures. A dubious guide, no doubt, too personal, too idiosyncratic, too bold an Ariadne. But why should he follow her clues when he had his own? (He thought of his own attempts at drawing as a boy, the heads he had sketched in his notebooks. Color was to the eye what dancing was to the body, but form appealed to him more. And sculpture more than painting, the archaic grandeur of the age when the Greeks were at one remove from the Egyptians. He loved those block-like images, before freedom had become too free.) And how honest Margaret was, and what sympathy she felt with the artist in his protest against the deformities of common life! For months, thanks to Margaret, his world had been colored with the genius of the Greeks and Italians. She had made him warmly aware of so much in his nature that was still quiescent.

As a good child of Boston, he wished to see the best in every kind—let nothing pass, unseen, unheard, that was excellent. Fanny Ellsler's dancing, for instance: could he ever forget this graceful silvery swimmer? The variety of her attitudes, the winning fun and spirit of her little coquetries, the beautiful erectness of her body? Or that slow, prolonged salaam?—she seemed to have invented new depths of condescension. What cheer and exhilaration the spectacle imparted! The sport and triumph of health, the virtue of organization. Such grace as hers, he knew, must rest on occult foundations of inward harmony.

But Dr. Peabody's shop was the likeliest haunt in town. They had all the new foreign books there, George Sand, Schleiermacher, Manzoni; you could stop and chat for a while, then carry off the latest German or French review. And there you were sure to meet the illuminati, talking and strolling about, or browsing over the counters: Dr. Channing and Washington Allston, perhaps, the veterans, or George Ripley, or Hedge, or those two grave suitors of the Peabody girls, Horace Mann and the shy Nathaniel Hawthorne. Ripley was collecting translators for his "Specimens of Foreign Literature," and Hedge was full of German metaphysics. There was always something in the wind at Dr. Peabody's. A boon, that house, for a country scholar for whom a new person was ever a great event.

One could linger there by the hour, then saunter off with some other casual visitor. Washington Allston, for instance: how appealing this old man was, so fragile, so quaintly courteous, with his glowing eyes and his silvery curls! Yes, and that legendary mission—to restore the grand manner of the sixteenth century, as his friend Coleridge had put it. A painter in the great line, as one couldn't but feel, a boulder of the European ledge, a spur of the Apennines of Titian and Michaelangelo, cropping out here in this remote America, unlike anything around it, and so far from reaching its natural elevation. He rose at ten o'clock, it was said, each morning, left his poor little house, with a pitcher of water in his hand, hurried through the dusty streets to his bleak little studio, sat down and smoked and contemplated his picture, then painted for a while and laid aside his brushes, and contemplated his picture again till dark. "Belshazzar's Feast" was the picture —that accurst, that baleful picture!—and for twenty years he had worked on it, in vain. He had started it in London, in the days of his renown: the subject had grown hateful, the mechanical labor was too great for him, he had had to change the perspective, and now he was white and feeble and the picture still unfinished.

(His townsmen had bought it in advance; the newspapers constantly talked of it; the public was agape for it. Could he disappoint the world?) He had put aside everything else for the sake of that picture, commissions, new attempts, peace of mind; but how winning the old man was, as he rambled across the bridge to his house in Cambridgeport! A poet too: he would take you into the studio, and place you before the picture, and recite to you in an undertone lines that had taken shape in his mind as he painted.

Boston might not be nobly mad, either for learning or philosophy, art or association; but who could think ill of a town that harbored such souls as this? Not Emerson; and the times were crescent. No doubt Allston had starved there, had fed upon himself, withered away in the wind, he in whose veins the South had run so warm. His friend Dana was right; his spirit had risen and soared, but without force, for Boston had afforded him "no combat with other intellects, no strife for mastery, which gives vigor and development to the mind." But the scene was changing fast—with all those bubbling wits at Dr. Peabody's! And Margaret's "Conversations" in that same engaging house. For Margaret was holding classes for the ladies of Boston, in Mythology, Ethics, Literature, "What is Life?" Why should their minds be so woolly, so wanting in precision and clearness? So vague, so cold, so provincial, in a world so full of delights? What pursuits were they fitted for, how could they use their means, what were they born to do and how should they do it? Coals for Margaret's fanning! Too many local interests! They should fix their minds on the broad, the objective, the tangible—"serious without being solemn, playful as well as deep." The ladies were disturbed to be told that in Christian times heathen Greeks should be envied, and they found it difficult to talk. But Margaret stirred them up, and they were soon aglow. They shook the films from their eyes; they melted, they laughed, they could scarcely express their rapture; and they showered their love and their gifts at the sibyl's feet.

Who could withstand that verve, that haughty assurance? Those endearing perceptions, that all-attaching eye? It was easy to laugh at Margaret; but who could dispute her vitality? Had she not given tongues to the dumb and grace to the awkward? And Boston was full of these voices, if one knew where to find them. There was Father Taylor, for one, the apostle to the sailors, a master of wild rhetoric, an unconscious artist. A dancing drunkard of his wit, and Emerson delighted in him. Occasionally, in the days of his pastorate, he had had this minstrel in his pulpit, and he could always count on a thrill when he threaded the crooked old waterside streets and dropped in at the Seaman's Bethel. What teeth and eyes this man had, like a jaguar's, or an Indian's! What authority, wilful and despotic, as he rode on the waves of the sunny ocean of his thought! He would weep and grieve and pray and chide in a tempest of passionate speech, and never break the perfect propriety with a single false note.

A man with a way and sweep like a frigate's way, that takes up the centre of the sea and paves it with a white street! (Another Robert Burns, this Father Taylor. No corpse-cold Unitarian. Mighty Nature's child!) And Sampson Reed was always ready for a chat. (The Swedenborgian druggist, who had written "The Growth of the Mind.") A grand poet, Swedenborg, a stark Scandinavian Berserker with an iron training; and who could discourse on the subject better than Reed? But he wouldn't admit it was poetry; he meant you to take it all for literal fact. . . . But really, Mr. Reed, those devils: you don't imagine. . . ?" But he did: those devils were solid flesh and blood.

One personage caught Emerson's fancy above all the others. On a June day in 1836 he turned in at the Masonic Temple, where Bronson Alcott's school was in its third year. He had met Alcott before and felt the attraction of this tall, blue-eyed prophet with his corn-colored locks and his open, courtly manner; but the school was a revelation. The beautiful, spacious room, the Gothic windows, the busts of Shakespeare and Plato, the well-chosen pictures on the wall, the gracious master presiding from his desk in the corner were very different from the dark, formal class-rooms that he had known as a boy. But what struck the visitor most was the conversation in progress between the master and the pupils. With what absorbed attention these diminutive Bostonians listened and responded! No suggestion of painful tasks, routine, irritation, severity. This teacher, with his dialectic method of query and answer, was a Socrates indeed, for whom questions of thought and taste were independent of age. He was like the sun in April warming into life a hive of torpid bees.

Emerson had found a friend, the reasonable creature he had always longed for. He had heard much of this dreamer who thought the world was to be redeemed by education and who had aroused such furious opposition in Boston.

A strange story was Alcott's. The son of a Connecticut farmer and mechanic, he had known the rigors of a primitive country school and had been set to work at fourteen in a clock-factory, the pride of a neighboring town. He had wandered to the South as a pedlar, with a small tin trunk in his hand and the hope of discovering a school in Virginia or the Carolinas where the rudiments he had learned at the rod's end would provide him with the work to which he felt predestined. He walked, he travelled about with horse and wagon, selling almanacs and tinware, thimbles, scissors, picture-books for children, spectacles, razors, buttons. Then, finding the South apathetic, he returned to Connecticut, where his uncle, Dr. Bronson, directed an Academy, and there, and at Germantown and Philadelphia, he opened schools and began to develop his methods. (No corporal punishment. Gymnastic exercises. No parrot-spelling of columns of unknown words. No treating these children as buckets to be filled with the barren knowledge of the world, but a veritable leading-forth of the natural disposition.) At last he had come to Boston for the great venture of his life. He had stirred up a storm of abuse, with his heterodox Conversations on the Gospels; for who was he to brush aside so lightly, with his pagan-Greekish talk of the beauty of the natural instincts, the hallowed Puritan dogma of original sin? ("The blissful moments," said Alcott, "are those when a man abandons himself to the Spirit. The highest duty is musical and sings itself. And children are so attractive because they are still under the sway of instinct.") But he had found a powerful ally in Dr. Channing, who shared these intimations, and he seemed to be winning his way.

A true comrade-in-arms. Emerson was entranced with him. He could read his Plato now with new eyes, for here was a Plato in the flesh. What was it the sage had said?—that "education should be conducted with a serene sweetness, never by force or violence, but by gentleness, accompanied with persuasion and every kind of invitation." Alcott's way, exactly! And behold, from his face too, as from the face of those divine ancients, there shone a pleasing mildness; and over his whole external form was diffused that air of dignity and ease, of affability and modesty, which, according to Plotinus, true wisdom, deeply possessed, gives to the manners. None of those smug arts, beloved of the worldlings of Athens and Boston, but the grace of the Muses. And what a gift for awakening aspiration and contemplation! He had, it was true, some rather odd ideas, as, for instance, that the human head was going to slough the body: the trunk would perish and the brain would unfold a new and higher organization. (He could hardly expect women to like such notions.) And he talked high and wide, and expressed himself very happily, and forgot all he had said: he seldom finished a sentence, but revolved in spirals until he was lost in the air. And his writing was vague and trite. He had never wrought his fine clay into vases, or his gold-dust into ingots; he played with his thought too much, without subduing it; he used too many phrases about the "Spirit" that he ought to have left to the Unitarian Association. But who was more candid than Alcott? Who liked one's bluntness better? And how he loved life and the present hour! No skulker, ready to nestle into any cast-off shell and form of the past. An apostle and a pilgrim. If Boston refused to hear him, he would take his staff and go among the people, walk through the country, discoursing to the school-teachers and holding conversations in the villages.

Such were the rewards when Emerson left his study and slipped into town for the day. His mind, in Alcott's company, kindled and burst into flame. With men like this walking the streets, who could complain of the dumbness, the pomposity of Boston? Then why not improve the occasion and form a club? Hedge would enjoy it, the ever-liberal Hedge, who was publishing his translations of the new German authors, and Orestes Brownson, French-and-Indian Brownson, who had opened a radical church for mechanics and laborers, and Theodore Parker, of course, that blue-eyed Friar Tuck of theologians, with his pug nose and his hearty grip, who was able to carry a barrel of cider in his hands, yes, and with twenty languages on the tip of his tongue. (Persian, Coptic, Syriac, Dutch, think of it!—and all wrapped up in the frame of a Yankee farmer. A glutton of learning, for all his ruddy face: he could scarcely be brought to admit that Hedge was "learned in spots." And a real bringer of good tidings. What New England pulpiteer had ever before praised the Lord for the voiceless fish, "moving with the flapping of the sea," for the "bunchy and calumniated toad" and the frog, "shaking the bog with his hoarse thunders"?) One could certainly count on Parker, that hierophant of Nature and muscular man. And George Ripley, and John Sullivan Dwight, with his cult of Mozart and Beethoven, and James Freeman Clarke, on his annual visits from Louisville. (He found it so "flat" out there, beyond the mountains. But he had carried Boston with him; he was toiling away at Greek, geology, mineralogy; he had started a magazine, the "Western Messenger." And the leaves of the cottonwood trees were "always in motion.") Good timber for a club. Unitarian ministers, for the most part, and mostly from habit and inertia, in their early thirties, with little taste for preaching and bursting with profane passions for poetry, music, painting or the Church of Rome. (John Dwight was the type of them all, Dwight who awoke on the Sunday after his ordination and remembered that he had prepared neither of his sermons for the day. Too much Mozart in his cosmos, together with a "certain want of fluency in prayer.") Every rustic manse within walking, running, racing distance of Boston would contribute a rill to the stream of good talk. Why stick at home and read Sir William Jones' life, or the life of Gibbon, to shame yourself into an emulating industry, when all these cordial souls were so eager to shame one another?

Why indeed? Whatever your studies might be, they would certainly thrive better for a little airing. Did your reading grow stale as you frowsted over your fire? How quickly the faded colors revived in the presence of that fellow-student who showed such a lively interest in your speculations! There was nothing like matching wits to restore the price of thought. A club then, by all means. The Symposium, perhaps. Or the Transcendental Club. A little starchy, this word, a little cold and stiff, Emerson said to himself. The Greeks would never have liked it: their thought needed no Transcendental bush, and they lived the *thing* as naturally as they breathed. But the word was a good flag to fly in the face of all this Boston Whiggism. Was man made to live like a pedlar, with his hand ever on his pocket, cautious, calculating? Or to nourish himself on the thin porridge and cold tea of Unitarianism? Or to take his revelation ready-made from a book bound in black cloth? Man, enthusiastic man, possessed by a god? Away with all this "evidence of the senses"! Let them say, if they like—with a wave of the hand—that Transcendentalism means "a little beyond." A little *within,* good friends, a little within!

The neophytes assembled, first four, then a dozen or so, now at Willard's Hotel in Cambridge, now at Brownson's house in Chelsea, or at Ripley's, or in Emerson's study in Concord. The neophytes assembled and took their seats.

Was the air a little frosty? Was the talk a little staccato? Were the voices a little sepulchral? Were the pauses long and frequent? They could only meet, these minds, by soaring up in the fog, fortunate if, in the course of an anxious evening, two of them came within hailing distance of each other.

Alas, it was all a pale, frail mist! One doesn't learn to loosen one's tongue in a lonely country parsonage; and the subjects—for instance, the Highest Aim—were not exactly enlivening. How chagrined the philosophers felt as they munched their russet apples, when the dish was handed round at the end of the soirée, and they vanished into the night! What wild comets of thought had whirled through their heads! What daring and extraordinary things they were on the point of saying!—and just as their blood was up it was time to go. That infernal Boston frigidity! They ought to have called it the Lonely Club. (With a seal: two porcupines meeting with all their spines erect, and the motto, "We converse at the quill's end.")

But they stuck it out. They had made up their minds to be genial, cost what it might. One evening Father Taylor came to the rescue: with his green spectacles thrown up on his forehead, he burst into a stream of indignant and sorrowful eloquence on the indifferentism of the churches and the lukewarm spirit of the day. And occasionally they happened on a topic that warmed them all like wine. Did property fulfil some natural need of man? Should they speak as they felt in the pulpit, or speak with reference to the fears and the sleep of others? Or the Union, the Constitution: how soon would Americans realize that individual character and culture were sacred, that these mass-obligations were trivial beside them? Or the state of affairs at Harvard. Everything was permitted in Cambridge that pleased the respectables, while that which the college existed for—to be a Delphi uttering oracles to elevate and lead mankind—*that* it was not permitted to be or to think of. But one topic especially stirred the club: the American Genius, the causes that hindered its growth. On this titanic continent, with nature so grand, why should genius be so tame? One had only to think of Bryant—chaste and faultless, but uncharacterized. Or Dr. Channing's preaching, the sublime of calculation. Allston was thin, and Greenough was thin, and Irving and Prescott and Bancroft. Not one drop of the strong black blood of the English race! No teeth and claws, no nerve and dagger. A pale, diluted stream.

There was the topic of topics: the lukewarm spirit of the day, as Father Taylor called it.

Who cared whether Bryant wrote good poems or not? Whether Greenough made a good statue? The great poems had been confessions of the faith of races, the great statues had been worshipped. No necessity of the people called these Americans out. And alas, why look for art where society was unbelieving, honeycombed, hollow? When society tingled with earnest zeal, beauty would be born. And why rail and complain in the meantime? Why not take some positive step, why not start a quarterly journal? With Alcott's title, *The Dial?* (He had used it for his private diary.) And Margaret Fuller as editor? (For Margaret herself had been present at some of the meetings, and what a gift she had for inspiring confidence! She had fused the chilly philosophers into a glowing company; she had felt the moods of the speakers, gathered their rays to a focus, seized their balloons of thought and pulled them back to the earth. And who knew as Margaret knew it the silent army of the younger generation, that throng of eager souls, in college and village, lonely, constrained, obscure, who had given in their adherence to the spiritual revolution?)

Trust Margaret to sound the reveille! Trust Margaret to fill *The Dial* with the burning thoughts of the young!

II

THE DIAL, CONCORD

IT was 1841, and Henry Thoreau had joined the Concord household. As a steward, an adopted son, a master of rural arts— chiefly, perhaps, to give Emerson lessons in gardening. He had his little room at the head of the stairs and worked, when he chose, about the yard and barn, banked up the fruit-trees against the winter and the mice, looked out to see when a pale was loose in the fence or a nail dropped from its place, set up the stoves and put the shutters to rights. There was never such a man for locks and hinges and door-knobs, or for making the chickens behave.

It was all in a family way, for Emerson had known Henry since he was a boy. He had helped him to get a scholarship at Harvard, for Henry's father, the pencil-maker on Main Street, was always short of money. And then he had had a surprise: Henry had come back to

Concord the walking incarnation of all his own ideas. He had steeped himself in the Greek and Roman sages, he had hunted out the Elizabethan poets, Fletcher, Drayton, Raleigh, whom Emerson especially loved. But this was incidental. He proposed to live without following any profession, live for the sake of living and keep alive by whatever means might offer. Live like a monk, if need were, live like a workman; earn his dollar a day by carpentering, gardening, painting. But live for his thoughts, his perceptions, his journal and his flute.

Emerson set to work, with this stern instructor, digging and hoeing in the garden. Not for long, to be sure; he found himself sadly untuned. The smell of the plants drugged him and robbed him of energy, and he soon awoke from his dream of chick-weed and red-root and made up his mind that writing and practical farming could never go together. But lessons in the art of walking, in the art of observing and exploring, were another matter, and Henry knew the country like a fox or a partridge; and, although he had no walks to throw away on company, he could always spare an afternoon for Emerson. He was not an easy companion, for he wanted a fallacy to expose or a blunder to pillory, he required a roll of the drums, a sense of victory, to call his powers into exercise. He would say, and wait for Emerson to contradict him, that nobody dared to walk to the Concord post-office with a patch on the knee of his trousers. Or that nothing was to be hoped from him or anyone if this bit of mould under his feet was not sweeter to him to eat than any other in the world or in any world. But only as long as the village was still in sight: in the swamps and pastures he forgot the sorry human race. And then what an air came over him, what a light shone in his eyes, and what magic Henry performed with the jackknife and spyglass and microscope that were tucked away in his pockets with his diary and pencil! Snakes coiled round his leg, fishes swam into his hand, a sparrow even alighted on his shoulder. He would name the plants that ought to bloom this day, and there they were, as if his voice had evoked them. He would hazard a guess that the spot where they were standing had once been an Indian camping-ground, then stoop and dig in a circle and uncover the blackened stones of an ancient fireplace. Emerson could easily believe him when he said that if he awakened from a trance in the depths of the forest he could tell the time of year within two days by the plants that were growing about him.

He was writing too, as diligently as Emerson: crowded little poems, in the manner of the seventeenth century, with a certain intricate melody. But his journal was the greatest delight —pastoral as Isaak Walton, it seemed to Emerson, spicy as flag-root, broad and deep as Menu. What prose Henry wrote, how acute were his senses! Half the wisdom of the ancients seemed to have been born again in this Concord Pliny. He was very severe with himself and shaped his rambling thoughts into formal essays with infinite toil and a good deal of hesitation. But when Emerson read his paper, "A Winter Walk," he was ready to account Henry the king of American lions.

They had not been friends very long when an opportunity came for them to work together in a more congenial way. Emerson was asked to take charge of *The Dial*. The magazine was not prospering, in spite of heroic efforts, and Margaret was unable to carry it any longer. There were scarcely one hundred subscribers. Some readers complained of the lack of a definite aim; others, that it savored too much of the old order of things. The reformers were annoyed by its literary pretensions, and those who cared for style were annoyed by the reformers. Margaret's idea had been to allow all kinds of people to say their say, without too much regard for their manner of saying it; and Emerson had winced at the barbarous form of some of the compositions. But Elizabeth Peabody had agreed to take over the management and find another printer; and if Henry would only canvass for new subscribers and Emerson would select the contents, they might make the paper a success in spite of all.

So *The Dial* came to Concord, and Henry read the proofs (and enlarged the list of subscribers to two hundred and twenty). Margaret had not been mistaken in promising the richest harvest of contributions. Her own paper on Goethe and her "Short Essay on Critics" were the best she was ever to write. There were Alcott's Orphic epigrams and Dwight's papers on music, poems by Christopher Cranch and William Ellery Channing, the doctor's nephew. There were sonnets by Jones Very and James Russell Lowell, who had spent a few months in Concord not long before. And Ripley and Parker, of course, and James Freeman Clarke had much to say. But the greatest surprise was the number of unknown writers who rallied about the paper as if they had found their natural home at last. There were fragments of private diaries, each with a note of distinction, comments on works of art, revealing some personal taste, sketches of village life, confessions, dialogues, soliloquies. *The Dial* was plainly a comfort and encouragement for dozens of lonely souls who felt themselves without support in the world.

Too "spirit-like" in expression. Carlyle was undoubtedly right. "Too aeriform, aurora-borealis-like. I can do nothing with vapors," he had written, after reading the earlier numbers, "I can do nothing with vapors but with them *condensed.*" Too much unbalanced intellectuality. But Thoreau was solid enough, and Parker and Dwight and Channing. And what unsuspected wealth *The Dial* revealed in the depths of this dumb New England! What reserves of thought and feeling! A chilly, misty dawn of some golden summer to follow.

What interested Emerson most, for it seemed to give most promise, was the poetry. He published some of the verses he was writing himself, "The Sphinx," "Wood-notes," "Saadi," and a few of his own essays; and he made a point of printing as much of Thoreau as possible. He reviewed the new books that struck him as most significant, Borrow's "Bible in Spain," Tennyson's Poems, "Two Years Before the Mast," by his old pupil Dana, and Browning's "Paracelsus." And he and Henry selected for publication passages from the Eastern Scriptures, Vishnu Sarma's "Amicable Instructions," the Chaldaean Oracles, the Analects of Confucius. (All unknown in America.) Then, at the end of the fourth year, as *The Dial* seemed to have made no further headway, the editor closed his desk. He stored away the remaining copies in the attic. (Where they lay for thirty years. In 1872 they were sold to the ragman.)

William Ellery Channing, the doctor's nephew and namesake, had come to Concord to live. He had married Margaret Fuller's sister, the pretty sister Ellen, and together they had taken the little Red Lodge a mile up the turnpike. Ellen (as cool and *dégagée* as Margaret was volcanic) had opened a school in the village, and Ellery was determined to work his acre of land.

A character, a true original, this Ellery Channing. He had published several pieces in *The Dial*—poems, "Ernest and the Seeker"—and Emerson had been eager to meet him. But Ellery was always playing hole-and-corner, tearing back and forth to the Western prairies or hiding at "Aunt Betty Atkins's" in Newburyport. With the manners of a man of the world and features that suggested all the Boston families with which he was connected, Ellery was as much the social antinomian as Henry Thoreau himself. He had refused to take his degree at Harvard and had built himself a log hut in the wilds of Illinois: he was resolved to have no commerce with the "bottomless stupidity" of the Bostonians. A poet, a botanist, a lover, as he said, of old books, old garrets, old wines, old pipes, an amateur in all things, he lived for the hour and chiefly for conversation.

No one so moody as Ellery. He was harsh and tender by turns, abrupt, disagreeable, distant, then cordial and generous. But who was a better crony for a walk? Ellery led like an Indian. Was Emerson piqued by the impatience of his countrymen, each one striving to get ahead of the rest? A stroll with Ellery soothed his irritation. He would stop by a clump of goldenrod: "Ah, here they are! These things consume a great deal of time. I don't know but they are of more importance than any other of our investments." He spent his mornings (for the farm was soon forgotten) conning old folios of his favorite authors: there was never a man of more recondite learning, with so many mottoes, conceits and allusions bubbling in his brain. His taste was so sound that if he said, "Here's a good book," Emerson knew he had a day longer to live; and if he preferred Herrick, as a true Greek, to Milton (who reminded him of his uncle Dr. Channing)—so much the better. Herrick, poet of cherries and Maytime, with his hen Partlett and his Julia's hair, was the right touchstone for strollers in rural Concord. And Ellery had such a wonderful respect for mere humors of the mind. He caught the most delicate shades of one's meaning, matched one's happiest phrase with another and always returned to the weather and politics when there was the least faltering or excess on the high keys. Capricious, yes, the April day incarnated and walking, soft sunshine and hailstones, east wind and flowery south-west by fits and starts. He complained of Nature—too many leaves, too windy and grassy. And he forgot one's existence for weeks, ceased to bow as he passed, then called and hobnobbed again as if nothing had happened. But a sensible, solid, well-stored man was Ellery, for all his whimsies. He despised door-yards with foreign shrubs. He said that trouble was as good as anything else if you only had enough of it. He admitted that even cows had their value. They gave the farmers something to do in summertime, and they made good walking where they fed.

    A perfect companion, Ellery, for a ramble

to White Pond, that pretty little Indian basin where Emerson could almost see the sachem canoeing in a shadowy cove; or to Flint's Pond, perhaps, or Nine Acre Corner. Sometimes Henry joined them, and then the bluebird's warble and the murmur of the brook would be drowned in the play of their talk: strokes of wit, tags of rhyme and the Latin names of the flowers, for Linnaeus, too, was one of the gods of Concord. They thought of those "herborizations" at Upsala, when the master summoned his class for an excursion into the country and they gathered plants and insects, birds and eggs, and returned in the evening, marching through the streets of the town with flowers in their hats, to the sound of drums and trumpets. Less pomp attended their own perambulations, but they were not less joyous. They lingered over every pool by the roadside, stopped to examine the buds of the marsh-marigold, tossed stones into the river and watched the circles and dimples and lovely gleaming motions of the water, for time meant as little to them as it meant to old weather-beaten Goodwin, fishing from sun-up to dusk on the bank. They discussed the labors of the farmers whose fields they passed, and the religion of the Indians, so much clearer and fresher, as Henry said, than the desiccated theologies of the paleface, and Shakespeare and Carlyle, Ebenezer Hubbard's pears and the architecture of Palladio, while Ellery's dog Peter, with his cheerful tail, capered through hedge and bush. Nor was the day complete till they had stripped and had their swim, now on the leafy little beach at Fairhaven Bay, now from some willowy ledge at Walden.

For a longer journey, to Sudbury, for instance, they could set out in Emerson's Jersey wagon, stopping wherever they chose: the good mare Dolly could be trusted to stand patiently for half a day at a tree while they roamed about in the woods and pastures. There was nothing like Sudbury meadows on a sunny morning to remind one of Isaak Walton's gentle Lea. The mere sight of Sam Haynes, fishing at the mouth of the Pantry Brook, was enough to set the rhymes running in one's head, rhymes as sweet as Carew's or Suckling's, sweet as the notes of the redwings and bobolinks that flitted over the fragrant marsh. From afar came the faint sound of the bells of Framingham. They pushed on to the hill for a glimpse of Marlboro. What a spectacle of rustic plenty and comfort, what ample farms, what mountains of pumpkins, what spacious houses, with squashes ripening between their Grecian columns! Gates's, where

Dr. Channing used to retreat, was no longer an inn; but they could picnic in the chestnut grove.

Now their goal was the Three Friends' Hill overlooking Concord, when the odor of grapes filled the breeze and the freedom of an orchard was dearer far than the freedom of all the Romes. Now it was the goose-shore swimming-place on the Assabet, or Baker's Farm, that sumptuous park—if only its owner had known his wealth!—with lawns and slopes and terraces like another Lord Breadalbane's; or Conantum, named by Ellery from its ancient master Eben Conant, a noble seigniory fit for some Yankee Montaigne. Not Shakespeare himself had sung a lovelier prospect—and what bard was to save this present beauty from oblivion? If Ellery could only have written as he talked, if, writing, he had not been so shamelessly indolent and slovenly, New England would have had its Virgil, for his mere presence turned the day into the most melodious of eclogues.

An art, walking, like any other, with strict qualifications: endurance, plain clothes, old shoes, an eye for Nature, good humor, curiosity, good speech, good silence and nothing too much. No loud singing, no story-telling, no vain words (Emerson said to himself) profaning the river and the forest. With a loved and honored companion his sentiments appeared as new and astonishing as the lightning out of the sky: every thought rushed to light, rushed to body, and society was already revolutionized. By himself Emerson was inclined to stop and linger. With Ellery and Henry walking was another matter: no graceful idling then, but a strenuous chase, for walking was Henry's work. One stepped along more quickly, submitting to one's guide; and the tempo of one's talk, so often languid, soon grew as brisk as the biting autumn air. Even when Henry stopped to study some plant by the pathside one felt the relentless ticking of his brain. It was always in action, that brain, hard, precise, clear as a seven-day clock.

Ellery too was hard, hard and cool, and Emerson liked him for it, he who liked dry light and hard clouds, hard manners and hard expressions. But Ellery could melt as well and waken to the most genial mirth. He was full of amusing notions. He suggested setting up in every village a magnified dollar as big as a barrel-head, made of silver or gold. Let Colonel Shattuck, he said, or some other priest be appointed to guard it; they would then have a local deity and could bring it baked beans and other offerings and perform rites before it. He was always laughing at the villagers and their stodgy ways, the passengers on the train squeezing their bundles and the member of the Legislature hastening to drain the last drop of gossip from the ginger-beer newspaper before he left the car to fodder and milk his kine. And he railed at Concord, he said he would rather have settled on the icy peak of Mount Ararat: it was absolutely the worst spot in the world. ("Think of the climate of Venice," he lamented, "of Cuba, the Azores, Malaga"—there was scarcely a field in Concord he had not watered with his tears.) Then he talked about landscape-painting, the only art that was worth a moment's attention.

So Ellery sauntered along, squandering his jewels as if they were so many icicles, sometimes not comprehended, sometimes not even heard. Henry was bleak beside him, bleak as frosty November. (But what a tonic! Even his captious paradoxes kept Emerson's wits in motion. Was he rather inclined to dream and drift? Henry, with a volley of facts, brought him back to the earth.) As they lingered beside some spring, Henry would take out his notebook and scribble away, with a mind fixed upon what he called the particular and the definite. Then Ellery followed suit and tried to recall his impressions, but all in vain. He soon slipped the notebook into his pocket again, or scrawled some sketch on the broken page, or contented himself with a few "ideal remarks."

Concord, congenial Concord! It was good to exchange ideas with artists and teachers, people of the city and the world. But how much Emerson learned from his country neighbors too! From the laborers, for instance: to refresh himself with the bone and sinew of society he had to avoid the so-called respectable classes as carefully as a good traveller in a foreign land avoids his own countrymen. Now and then, at least. Take a group of villagers laying a new bridge. How close they were to their work! They sympathized with every log and anticipated its every stir with chain and crowbar. And how grand were their postures, their air, their very dress!—like figures of Michaelangelo. No other cultivation but that of war could have made such forms and carriage.

He lingered by a blacksmith or a truckman. No fear these men would speak because they were expected to speak; they were realists, not dictionaries, and they only uttered words that stood for things. The style of the Boston scholars was so trite and poor because language was properly made up of the spoils of actions, of trades, arts, games, metaphors borrowed from natural and mechanical processes, from the street and the field and the market. That was Plato's secret: if he loved abstract truth, he drew his illustrations from sources disdained by the polite, from mares and puppies and pigs, from potters, horse-doctors, butchers, fishmongers and cooks. Everett and Bancroft should certainly have lived in Concord. They would never have poured out such floods of empty rhetoric if they had spent a few minutes in the square each morning listening to the drovers and teamsters. What rattling oaths, how beautiful and thrilling! They fell like a shower of bullets. What stinging phrases, and that fiery double negative! No pale academicisms there, but a strong, salty speech, brisk and laconic, words so vascular and alive that they would bleed if you cut them, words that walked and ran.

Where could Emerson pass an hour better than on the Mill Dam, dropping into the grocery and the Squire's office, or chatting with Sam Staples on the steps of the court-house? Or walking along beside Edmund Hosmer as he ploughed his cornfield? Sam alone, with his liberal experience, as hostler, bar-keeper, constable, deputy-sheriff, as jailor, auctioneer and real-estate agent, was a veritable Sancho Panza for any Don Quixote of the pen. And Edmund Hosmer was a Caesar, an Alexander of the soil, conquering and to conquer. A victor, this faithful, sweet-tempered man, the hero, in his old weather-worn cap and blue frock bedaubed with the slime of the marsh, of six thousand daily battles, and standing, with Atlantic strength and cheer, invincible still. (Sometimes, when Edmund Hosmer was not too tired, he would drop in for an evening in Emerson's parlor, and what weight and actuality he contributed to the talk! Especially when Alcott was there, the winged Alcott, like an astral body without visible hands and feet.) And a master was Abel Moore, that musician who could make men dance in all sorts of weather. Trees bore fruits for him that Providence never gave them, and grapes from France and Spain yielded pounds of clusters at his door. He could turn a bog into a meadow with a stroke of his instrument or cover a sand-hill with peach-trees and vines, and he the plainest, the stupidest-looking fiddler that ever drew the rosin over his bow.

They shamed one's slight and useless city limbs, these soldiers of the soil—shamed the slackness of a scholar's day. A glance over Abel Moore's fence, a half-hour in the field with

Edmund Hosmer, was a tonic for Emerson's will. And these men too spoke the language of nature. They challenged his mind, they drove his notions into a corner and obliged them to render up their meaning in a phrase, at the point of a pistol. They made him study the low tone, and he never forgot in their presence that the roots of the great and high must still be in the common life.

A capital place, Concord, for the study of human nature. He could find every human type there. Take Cardinal de Retz's Memoirs: it was easy to identify all his principal characters, playing similar parts in the village comedy. There was M. de Rohan, whose only talent was dancing and who knew that his element for rising in the world was the ball-room. And that old granny of a M. d'Angoulême, and Beaufort, who was only a private man and affected neutrality; and Mazarin, with his genius for going about the bush and giving to understand; and Mr. E—— of Bangor who never finished his sentence—"you take the idee?" In the country church one saw the cousins of Napoleon, of Wellington, of Wilberforce, Bentham, Humboldt. A little air and sunshine, an hour of need, would suffice to call out the right fire from these slumbering peasants. The more silently they sat in their pews the louder their faces spoke—of the plain prose of life, timidity, caution, appetite, old houses, musty smells, retrograde faculties "puttering round" in paltry routines from January to December. The old doctor was a gallipot, the bookbinder bound books in his face, and the landlord mixed liquors, in motionless pantomime. Emerson could scrutinize every breed in the germ and verify all the impressions his reading had given him.

Why should people talk so much of the broadening effect of travel? You made an immense conquest of humanity by studying one man thoroughly. And Juvenal was right: "A single house will show whatever is done or suffered in the world." All history—Parthia, Macedon, Rome and the Netherlands—repeated itself every year in Concord. At one end of the village scale were the clowns and sots who made the fringes of your tapestry of life and gave a certain reality to the picture: old Sol, old Moore, who slept in Dr. Hurd's barn, and the denizens of Bigelow's and Wesson's bar-rooms. At the other end was the court-house, where the greatest men in the country appeared and spoke, Channing and Everett and Choate, Wendell Phillips and Webster: the village got a handful of every ton of greatness that came to Boston.

And there were shows and processions, animal-trainers and conjurors, revivalists and reformers, tourists and politicians—not to mention the Penobscot Indians who always came back with the summer. You had only to mix your impressions with a little imagination, and the whole panorama of human life unfolded before your eyes.

A little imagination! Sometimes, at night, as Emerson lay awake, he listened to the endless procession of wagons creaking past his gate on the great road from Boston to the mountain villages of New Hampshire and Vermont. All the wealth and goods of the Indies, of China and Turkey, of England and Germany and Russia, were in those wagons, streaming through Concord. Easy for him then to remember that the whole world was to be found in any least part of it, that the stars and celestial awning that overhung his own walks and discourses were as brave as those that were visible to Coleridge as he talked, or Ben Jonson and Shakespeare, or Chaucer and Petrarch and Boccaccio when they met. One had only to make much of one's own place, and it became in actuality all that one's fancy desired.

It was true that the world came to you if you were ready to receive it, if some fact in your experience gave you the key. The more facts, the more keys: that was the beauty of living close to the concrete. Housekeeping was a universal school, where all knowledge was taught you, and the price of your tuition was simply your annual expense. You wanted your stove set up, and this want entitled you to call on the professors of tin and iron in the village, inquire the cost of production of cast and wrought metal, the kinds of iron they had, all the secrets of the trade. You wanted soap or vinegar, manure, medicine, and you played the chemist; you were a politician with the selectmen and the assessors, a naturalist with your trees, hens, wood and coal. You opened, in short, a shop in the heart of all crafts and professions. And besides, the familiar household tasks were agreeable to the imagination. Were they not the subjects of all the Greek gems?

Emerson was open in Concord—how easy it was to be open!—open at every pore to the common life. To the spring sounds in the village evenings; to the winning, artful-artless ways of the young girls in the shops, buying a skein of silk and gossiping for half an hour with the broad-faced shop-boy (each laying little traps for the attention of the other, and each jumping joyfully into the traps), to the casual talk of pot-hunters and wood-choppers and cattle-drivers, and the local worthies exchanging dry remarks round the grocery stove; to the amphibious, weather-beaten, solitary fishermen on the river, floating in their flat skiffs and consoling themselves with rum; to the farmer who found in Plato so many of his own ideas; to the Social Circle that met on Thursday evenings—doctor, lawyer, trader, miller, mechanic, solid men, yielding solidest gossip, like the circle in "Wilhelm Meister" of which every member was a master of some indispensable art; to the Indians on the river—they could give you a new tea every day, and a new soup, lily-soup, hemlock tea, tea from the snow-berry, and cut a string from spruce-root, something no white man could ever do; to old George Minott up there on the slope, in his little hip-roofed cottage, with his cow and his corn and his "crooknecks." . . .

Congenial Concord!

III

THE REFORMERS

THE reformers thronged the roads. The Chardon Street Convention in Boston in November, 1840, had assembled a thousand messiahs from the woods and mountains. There were Dunkers, Muggletonians, Agrarians, Abolitionists, Groaners, Comeouters. Every village cross-roads in New England had contributed a voice and a scroll.

They roamed about the countryside in long gowns and with hair over their shoulders, and many a strange apparition haunted Emerson's house. The vegetarians came, for whom the world was to be redeemed by bran and pumpkins; and those who would not eat rice because it was raised by slaves; and those who would not wear leather because it was stolen from animals; and those who rejected vegetables the roots of which grew downward (and food that fire had polluted). And they sat at Emerson's table and criticized or abstained. ("Tea? *I?* Butter? *I?*") They made his Thanksgiving turkey an occasion for a sermon; they lectured him over his mutton on the horrors of the shambles. They even invaded his study, these portents of the times, formidable, unanswerable. He sat there glued to his chair, all thought, all action, all play departed, paralysed. They somehow took the oxygen out of the air, and he twisted like the eel in the exhausted receiver.

The Phrenologists came too, and the Mesmerists, and the Homeopathists, and the Swedenborgians. And the Rat-hole Spiritualists whose gospel came by taps in the wall and thumps in the table-drawer—wizards that peeped and muttered. (A pistareen a spasm, or nine dollars for a fit.) What quaint phantoms were abroad in this morning of time! But among these maggoty souls there were other and more appealing figures, perplexed, ardent, hopeful, inarticulate. Edward Taylor, for instance, the journeyman printer: touching it was to hear of his little group of six youthful apostles who met one evening in Boston and talked over his plan for the abolition of money till all were convinced that nothing could contribute more to the brotherhood of man. (He had wandered all over the South, with a light in his eye, paying for his night's lodging with papers and tracts.) There were others, like those two young clerks who had forsaken their counting-houses and gone off to a hut in the woods: they had worked away through the winter reading and writing (in mittens), as best they could for the cold, and had barely escaped with their lives. New types, desires that had never been voiced before in prosaic America. What were they seeking, these young men, what were they feeling, thinking, for what were they groping?

For modes of life, perhaps, familiar enough in history, or in other parts of the world—in China, in India, in Paris, in the cells of the Thebaid, in studios and taverns of Moscow, Rome or London; for careers and social customs, outlets, disciplines, that a simple colonial society had never dreamed of providing, had not been able to provide. And withal they shared the faith of the Age of Revolutions, a faith like that of the first Christian age in the immediate perfectibility of man and society. (The Communists were on the march: every month some new colony was arriving from Europe, setting out to build its Eden in Ohio and Missouri.) No more compromises, no more adjustments, no more half-hearted acceptances of the merely customary. Trade was selfish and fraudulent, education mere word-mongering, politics a swindle and the Church a lie. On all hands the young were seceding from the social organization, discarding the forms that existed and seeking forms of their own.

No need to stir from Concord to see how the tide was turning. The village hummed with these plans. Brook Farm was an accomplished fact. Some time before George Ripley and Margaret Fuller had discussed the project in Emerson's study. It was charming, refreshing, engaging; and yet, at the name of a society, all his repulsions had played, his quills had risen and sharpened. He had wanted to be convinced, to be thawed, to be aroused by this new dawn of human piety to a mania better than temperance; but instead he had sat aloof, his voice had faltered and fallen. Was this the cave of persecution that might become for him the palace of spiritual power, this room as it were in the Astor House hired for the Transcendentalists? Should he raise the siege of his own hencoop and march baffled away to a pretended siege of Babylon? Could he work better than at home in that select, but not by him selected, confraternity? Toiling in the barnyard and the peat-bog, in a blue frock and cow-hide boots, certainly had its points, but it was the last form of activity to stimulate the mind. He had expressed himself very freely to the brave Ripley, but he had greatly enjoyed his visits to the community. Who would have dreamed that such grace, such a gay abandon, could have been evoked out of the old dry shell of Puritanism?

And now another plan was in the air. The dauntless Alcott had conceived the boldest scheme of all. He had passed through many vicissitudes, this God-intoxicated man. Boston had rejected him at last; his school was gone; his book had been remaindered and sold for trunk-linings. He had come to Concord, with his wife and children, and hired himself out as a wood-chopper. (Alcott, even so, who should have been maintained in a prytaneum. Alcott, who had so little genius for labor, preach it as he might. It cruelly wasted his time, it depressed his spirit to tears.) Then comforting news had reached him, as he toiled away at the chopping-block: the star that had sunk in the New World had risen in the Old. A school had been established in London, named in his honor and manned by his disciples. Alcott House, no less! The disciples had urged the master to make them a visit, and Emerson had collected a purse to cover his expenses. He had filled the purse himself, in fact—ten golden sovereigns and a bill of exchange on a firm of English bankers; and at last he had despatched the pilgrim with a handsome letter to Carlyle.

Then what should begin to appear at the little post-office window? Pamphlets, bundles of them, more than Concord had ever seen before. Pamphlets, periodicals, prospectuses, broadsheets, advertisements, and all stamped with the head of Queen Victoria. From Alcott's new associates! There were Communist Manifestos and Phalansterian Gazettes, plans for Syncretic Associations, Hydropathic Societies and Health Unions, Appeals of Man to Woman, treatises on the Necessity of Internal Marriage. Alcott had discovered an England that was never mentioned in travellers' books and had hastened to send the happy tidings back to his friend in Concord.

A letter presently followed. Alcott was coming home. Not alone; the masters of Alcott House, Charles Lane and Henry Wright, were sailing with him. The school had been driven to the wall, and they had all decided that the spirit of England was "hostile to human welfare, and her institutions were averse to the largest liberty of the soul." (In America, Alcott wrote, "is that second Eden to be planted, in which the divine seed is to bruise the head of evil and restore man to his rightful communion with God.") Emerson was troubled. How had Alcott pictured to these confiding Britons the paradise to which he was leading them? He despatched a hasty reply. . . . You must show it to your friends, Alcott. I say merely this, they can safely rely on your theories, but they must put no trust whatever in your statement of facts. . . . Alcott, the ever-candid, carried out these instructions. And now his victims, not to be deterred, were already on their way.

Six months later, in the little red house at Fruitlands, Alcott lay down upon his bed and turned his face to the wall. The Con-Sociate Family was a failure. How happy they had been, driving over in the big wagon from Concord, on that rainy June day, happy for all the rain, with the bust of Socrates on the front seat and the children laughing and chattering behind! Dreams of the Pythagorean life, of the school at Crotona, had swept the philosopher's brain as he hastened the horse. What dreams!— the morning walks in the grove, the searching discussion of doctrines and disciplines, the chaste repast of honey, maize and salad, the domestic labors and economies, the pure white garments, the gallant hospitalities, the bath and the evening meal and the quiet sleep. Once more the Grecian sun was to rise over the earth, amid the gracious meadows of Massachusetts, rise over a world redeemed by serenity and wisdom.

Emerson had watched the calamitous venture with a more than benevolent eye. For himself, he could only build on his own ground, unaided, his house of peace and benefit, good customs and free thoughts. But that was not Alcott's way, and there was always something right about Alcott's undertakings; so his heart and his purse were open to the rashlings—a deed for their land was made out in his name as trustee. They had chosen an enchanting spot for the community: a steep slope near the village of Harvard, with a view that spread over miles of well-tilled farms and well-pruned orchards. The house was amply stocked, with comely maple furniture, cupboards full of copper and brass, a library of a thousand volumes in the front entry. (What books! Pindar, Alcaeus, Mimnermus, Spinoza, Behmen, pagan and Christian poets, mystics, sages, the richest collection of its kind in all America—Lane's library brought from London.) At the foot of the slope was the twenty-acre field, redeemed from the curse of ownership, where they meant to cultivate their grain, pulse, herbs and flax, and their upright, aspiring vegetables, not with the enslaving plough, that bane of the republic of animals, but with the spade, the symbol of the creative life. No manure—Nature was not to be forced. No polluting animal food within doors. No tea or coffee to disturb the poise of the physical organism. Bread made from unbolted flour, and shaped, to render it palatable, in the forms of beasts. The men bathed in the brook, the women in a shelter of clotheshorses covered with sheets: Alcott himself mounted the ladder without and poured the water from a pitcher over their heads. For the rest, there was much emblematic ceremony. When the first load of hay was driven into the barn, one member of the household made a little speech: "I take off my hat, not that I reverence the barn more than other places, but because this is the first fruit of our labor." Then all fell silent for a time, that holy thought might be awakened. And on May Alcott's third birthday, the child was escorted by the whole community to the grove and crowned with flowers, while Alcott read an ode composed by himself in honor of his daughter.

But how could such an Academe endure? The British apostles quarrelled. Wright found the lack of butter, tea and coffee "too hard for his inside" and the regular hours and clearing up of scraps "too desperate hard for the outside." Young Isaac Hecker, already on the road to Rome, was unwilling to submit to a merely pagan discipline; and another member, a lady, was found to have eaten fish at a neighbor's house. (It was only the tail, she insisted, but out she went.) They had abjured the plough, but they failed to do the spading; and they would have had no crop if Joseph Palmer had not brought over his oxen from Leominster and set them to work at the last minute, while the rest of the Con-Sociate Family averted their eyes. They had planted their apple and pear-trees in the path of the north wind; and the men had drifted away on a lecturing tour when the grain was ready to be harvested. At last winter came and nothing was left but the stick of the beautiful rocket. (Nothing but Joseph Palmer and his yoke of oxen. Joseph Palmer remained; and for twenty years thereafter some fragrance of the original dream clung to this paradise lost. The house was a shelter for the hungry and the destitute; and two great iron pots, one containing baked beans and the other potatoes, always stood by the door ready for passers-by.)

Emerson had shared their hopes, and more than once he had come to the rescue of the innocents. (On that winter's day, for instance, when Joseph Palmer shovelled the snow off the road that led into Fruitlands and Silas Dudley shovelled it back again. The road crossed Silas's land—an endless cause of warfare, and for once neither of the old men would surrender: they had to send for Emerson to settle the dispute.) He had shared their hopes. How much he couldn't but say for all the reformers! It was true that their wish to obey impulse was guarded by no old, old Intellect, which knows metes and bounds. But that was their loss, not his, and what qualities they had, and how grateful he was to them for calling to his attention one by one all the problems of the time! The partial action of their minds in one direction was a telescope for the objects on which it was pointed. And they were enthusiasts too: where else could one look for that virtue in the circle of American wits and scholars?

There was much to be said for the reformers. They were right in refusing to adapt themselves to usages that had ceased to have any meaning. They were right in revolting against employments and standards that stifled their genius and their conscience. Right they were in asserting —and how clear they made it!—that the cost of life was almost all for conformity. (Intellect cost very little, the heart, beauty. Then why struggle so hard for money? "Do you think," said John Hunter, engrossed in dissecting a tiger, "do you think I can leave my work for your damned guinea?") And they alone were attempting, however blindly, to redeem the grand promises of the Revolution, they, and not the Cotton Whigs of State Street. Were they even so wrong in their disbelief in the Government? (What a pother, this, about Government! These caucuses, these conventions, with every palpitating heart swelling with the cheap sublime of magnitude and number! One had only to look at Kansas, at Mexico, Cuba—was the capital enemy of the comfort of all good citizens anything but this ugly Government? The politicians fancied that the popular laws had to be maintained by force. A pity they couldn't revoke their Government for a week, to save themselves the trouble, and watch the result. The popular laws, the laws of natural right, the laws of natural expedience! O fatuous politicians! You would find the priests and the lawyers, the bankers and chambers of commerce, the innkeepers, the village grocers, you would find the very farm-hands in the fields and the fishermen on the river mustering with fury to their support!)

Much to be said, even for the vegetarians.

Their ostentatious glasses of cold water, their dry, raw diet might well make one's blood run cold to see. No joyful signs that they had ceased to care for food in nobler cares. One might think intemperance better, with such a ruling love. But who argued so sourly for beef and mutton against these men of herbs and grains? The fat and ruddy eater who had just wiped his lips from feeding on a sirloin, whose blood was spouting in his veins and whose strength kindled that evil fire in his eye. It was not the voice of man one heard, but the beef and brandy roaring for beef and brandy. And were these to play the judge in their own cause?

How could Emerson shake his head and turn the reformers away?—the greatest heretic of them all? He could only applaud and envy (while his heart sank within him). When some zealot came and showed him the importance of the Temperance Reform, his hands dropped— what excuse could he offer? Then an Abolitionist described to him the horrors of Southern slavery. (He was certainly guilty, guilty!) A philanthropist told him of the shameful neglect of the schools by all good citizens. (Guilty, guilty again!) He heard of the poor, living on crusts and water, and he took to the confessional anew. He hadn't a leg to stand on. And he sat there, frigid, unhappy, convicted, laboring for speech.

That gulf, and those mendicant arms! That accusing bosom of his, that unanswering bosom! A yoke of oxen could have turned between every pair of words he was able to extort from it. Nothing to say, with so much that he ought to say? Who was the porcupine now? Who was on stilts? Was it true that he didn't belong to these people, that they didn't belong to him? They fled to him, each with a pet madness in his brain. They hastened to him with the utmost joy and confidence that they were the very souls his faith invited. Was he not the prophet of self-reliant action, the voice that affirmed their desires and justified their refusal to conform to the stale prescriptions of society? Who but he had painted those entrancing pictures of a life in harmony with nature, a free, spontaneous life like that of the Golden Age? They had flocked to hear him lecture, they had pored over his essays; and who but they had set out to make his gospel real? Had he nothing to say to them now, no word of cheer for their means and methods, no hand but that of a friendly neutral to lend them in actualizing their dreams of a better day?

Disturbing, these importunate reformers,

much more disturbing than the watch-dogs of the established order who had barked so fiercely at the prophet. What a power he had of begetting false expectations! He had blundered along for a time, assured by the surprise and joy of those to whom he communicated his results. Then he looked up for a moment, and the sympathy was gone or changed. The faces of all his friends were shaded with grief, and the bystanders accused him. (Come, soul, he said to himself, new solitudes, new marches! Jump into another bush and scratch your eyes in again! Pass on to new developments as surprising as your first, to fresh indirections and wonderful alibis that will dissipate the indictment!)

They had asked him to throw himself into their causes, to adapt his life to theirs. He was willing to try a few experiments, just to see if he could. Manual labor: to make it an "honest sweat," had he not arranged with Thoreau to teach him the real austerities of the hoe and the spade? He persuaded his wife to invite the Alcotts to join them and establish a new Fruitlands, *à quatre,* in Concord. He asked the housemaid and the cook to take their meals with the family. He breakfasted on bread and water. He adopted a vegetable diet. But the servants refused to leave the kitchen, and Mrs. Alcott declined to share in a second venture; the vegetarian experiment was half-hearted, and the manual labor was abandoned when Emerson found that it dulled his wits more than it toughened his nerves. Reform was not for him.

For Emerson had watched the reformers. He had noted the effect their activities had upon them. They were bitter, sterile people all too often. Their eyes were so filled with abstract images that the poetry of every day, the light shining in a child's spoon, the sparkle on a mote of dust, they saw not at all. And what egoists they were, how detached from the collective forces that kept life sane! They became tediously good in some particular, and negligent and narrow in the rest. They shared the new light that promised the kingdom of heaven, and they ended with champing unleavened bread and devoting themselves to the nourishment of a beard. The more they tried to impose their will upon others, to transform the external world, the more they fell out of relation with their own souls.

Not for Emerson was the sociable satisfaction of scaling with others the silver mountains whose enchantments he had sketched. He saw the peaks from the valley, but the moment he began to climb the vision vanished. And to see, to paint, to feel was his proper task. He would listen to no more reproofs but steadily persist in his own native choices against all argument and example—defend them against the multitude, defend them against the wise. Defend them against his disciples. By no man's distaste was he to be chidden out of his most trivial natural habit. Even pie for breakfast!

IV

AT WORK

COME, quit the high chair, he said to himself, lie down and roll on the ground. Enough of this playing tame lion and talking down to people! And a truce to these disputations!

"I am tired of fools," said his aunt, with wonderful emphasis. Where were the spade and the hoe? There was nothing like a bout in the garden for the sinking heart and the clouded brow, for the perturbation and fret of too much sitting. No harm if he worked at first with a little venom: that good hoe, as it bit the ground, avenged his wrongs, and he had less lust to bite his enemies. (Manual labor, at moments, had its value!) By smoothing the rough hillocks he smoothed his temper; by extracting the long roots of the piper-grass he drew out his own splinters. And before long he heard the bobolink's song and beheld the blessed deluge of light and color that rolled around him.

No need now to run for Acton Woods and live with the squirrels. The cranks and the bores were forgotten.

To every reproach he knew but one answer, to go again to his work. He had no genius? Then he would work the harder. He had no virtues, he neglected his relations—he would only work the harder. He had lost the esteem of all decent people, he must regain some position and relation: true as ever—he would work harder still. In his journals he had accumulated in the course of years a store of observations, reflections, perceptions. He jotted them down in various notebooks, paged and indexed according to their topics; then, when he wished to give a lecture, on the Poet, for instance, or Manners, he gathered together the material he had on the subject, arranged and combined it and added whatever suggested itself as he copied his entries out. The lectures were the basis of his essays, but they had to be re-handled. He condensed and pruned away the topical allusions, the anecdotes he had used to hold the attention of his audience; and he did what he could to organize his thought —not often with much success. Not for him was the laborious joy of the systematizer: he had often regretted it, but he had little power of construction. The sentence was his unit, at most the paragraph. For the rest, an apparent order was the best he could hope for, an order like that of his grand old sloven, Montaigne.

He had published little: "Nature," that first little book, written in the Old Manse, to the tune of the wind in the willow-tree that overhung his window (five hundred copies, many of them still unsold), the two volumes of "Essays," the "Addresses" of 1844. A relatively slight performance for a man of forty; but why should he rush into print? The good of publishing his thoughts was that of hooking to himself like-minded men and of giving to men he valued, Carlyle, for instance, Thoreau, Parker, Alcott, one stimulated hour. A single book well done contained the whole of his history. It was rhetoric—was it not?—that took up so much room; and the great thing was to charge a few lines with a world of meaning. Each sentence should be an idea, and every idea one that had filled his whole sky when he first conceived it. Most Americans, he felt, were over-expressed, beaten out thin, all surface without depth or substance. The thoughts that wandered through their minds they never absorbed or made flesh of; they reported them as thoughts, retailed them as stimulating news to all and sundry. At a dreadful loss they played this amusing game. For himself, he could hardly ponder his discoveries too much, digest them and turn them over in his mind. The writing should be like the settlement of dew on the leaf, of stalactites on the cavern wall, the deposit of flesh from the blood, of woody fibre from the sap.

He knew and would know no such thing as haste in composition. Well said Simonides: "Give me twice the time, for the more I think the more it enlarges"; and he who found himself hurried and gave up carrying his point, even for once, wrote in vain. Goethe had the *urkräftige Behagen,* the stout comfortableness, the stomach for the fight, and he would have it too! It was true that every writer was a skater and had to go partly where he wished and partly where the skates carried him. True that a thought he had once believed so happy often turned out to be nothing but empty words. While it glittered newly before him he fancied he had chipped off a scale of the universe; then he came again to the record a few months later and it seemed the merest tinsel. But certain things he could do to control his style, keep it hard and firm, hard but light and elegant as Landor's. He could cancel every "very," and every "intense" and "exquisite," avoid the fat of the language. (Had he used "grim" too often? A mannerism, perhaps; and that would never do.) He could keep to the Saxon forms and eschew the ponderous Latinisms; he could make every word cover a thing. And what compensations there were for all his difficulties! A new phrase at times was like a torch applied to a train of powder—it awakened so many thoughts. And sometimes in making a sentence he felt himself launching out into the infinite and building a road into Chaos and Old Night.

But how control his moods? They never believed in each other. One state of mind was never able to remember, was unable even to conceive of another state. Life was a flash of light, then a long darkness, then a flash again. Today the electric machine would not work, not a spark passed; and presently the world was all a cat's back, all sparkle and shock.

Mysterious, ungovernable, these periodic motions of the soul. There were fortunate hours when things sailed dim and great through his head, hours when the right words came spontaneously like the breath of the morning wind, when he could not sit in his chair for the joy that brought him bolt upright and sent him striding about the room, when he hadn't the composure to set down the thought that thrilled him. His intellect was so active that everything ran to meet it. He was like the maple trees in the spring when the sugar flows so fast that one cannot get tubs enough to contain it. And then came hours of pain, sterility, ennui, and he sat out the day and returned to the necessities of the household doubting if all this waste could ever be justified. No child passing the house on his way to school, no boy carrying a basket, but gave him a feeling of shame and envy. He was on the brink, it seemed, of an ocean of thought into which he could not swim. And sometimes the ocean itself seemed a mirage.

Was persistence enough, at such times, mere brute sitting, day after day, in the face of his own scepticism? It was true that the mood returned, sooner or later, always, and life had a grip again and the hours a taste. How cheering were those anecdotes of old scholars and poets, Niebuhr, for instance, whose divination came back to him after years of eclipse, and George Herbert who, having lost the muse in his youth, found himself later, "after so many deaths," living and versing again. He had known such minds himself, minds like those pear-trees which, after ten barren seasons, burst into a second and even more vigorous growth. But was there no way of domesticating these high states of contemplation and continuous thought? The rich veins of ore were always there, could he only command the shaft and draw them out. Writing was his metre of health, and success in his work was food and wine, fire and horse and holiday. Were there no tonics for the torpid mind, no rules for the recovery of inspiration?

Alas, neither by land nor by sea could one find the way to the Hyperboreans! But one thing was certain: his talent was good only as long as he worked it. If he ceased to task himself he had no thoughts. That was the value of the journal he kept so faithfully; every day he collected the disjointed dreams, the reveries, the fragments of ideas, the drupes and berries he found in his basket after endless and aimless rambles in woods and pastures. It was the hive in which he stored his honey, cell by cell, as the bees in his brain distilled it. A treasure, this journal, for a desultory mind; many were its uses. He could no more manage his thoughts than he could manage thunderbolts; but once he got them written down he could come and look at them every day and grow accustomed to their faces, and, by and by, discovering their family likeness, he could pair them and range them better and join them in the proper order. By this means too he could convert the heights he reached into a table-land. A fact that was all-important a month ago here stood along with one that was equally important a month before, and next month there would be another. Here they all occupied but four lines, and he could not read these thoughts together without juster views of each than when he read them singly. His journal was indispensable, for what was written was the foundation of a new superstructure, a guide to the eye for still another foundation. Every thought he expressed was a cube, and every cube a candidate for the mosaic of his essays. And if the results were precious, so was the habit. Work, of all tonics, was the most effective, and this was the most inviting form of work.

No doubt, but for work itself what were the best conditions? The free mind was the fruit of an austere law: it had to be reconquered day by day, it subsisted in a state of war and belonged only to those who fought for it. But how conduct the fight, how prepare for it? What were the omens, and how was he to read them? How coax and woo the strong instinct to bestir itself and work its miracle? The ancients were masters of this art: what was it Plato said about living out of doors and simple fare and gymnastic exercises, and Pythagoras, of the use of certain melodies to awaken in the disciple now purity, now valor, now gentleness? For every constitution there were certain natural stimulants, just as there were natural poisons, and the problem was to find these and regulate one's life accordingly.

For himself, he had such low animal spirits that he could not stand an extravagant, flowing life. He regretted it as much as he regretted the shortness of an American scholar's day. He marvelled at the constitution of the Germans, with their twelve, fourteen, sixteen hours of work. He loved in others the generous, spontaneous soil that flowered and brought forth fruit at all seasons. But he had to consult the poorness of his powers; he had to be content with moderate, languid actions. If he had obeyed his irregular impulses, established half the relations his fancy prompted, he would not have been followed by his faculties; he would certainly have died of consumption in six months. Parties disqualified him, and so did arguments. There were those who, disputing, made him dispute, and nervous, hysterical persons who produced the like symptoms in himself.

The one good in life was concentration, the one evil dissipation. What untuned him was as bad as what crippled or stunned him: domestic chores, even correcting proof-sheets, even packing a trunk. And talking about himself—how empty it made him feel! And being praised—a pest, the worst of all spoil-thoughts. (One turned around to look at oneself and one's day was lost in personal considerations.) Trifles? But a grasshopper was a burden. It was all very well to talk of a life taken as it comes. Thoreau, with his tough grain, knew the weight of these feathers in the scale: he had found that the slightest irregularity, were it only the drinking of too much water on the preceding day, disturbed the delicate poise that composition demanded. Carlyle knew this too, with his room on the top floor, high above the orbit of all housemaids: he could hope there for six years of history. And George Sand knew it, humoring her love of heat. Was the steel pen a nuisance? Try the quill. For himself, he pounded so tediously on that string of the exemption of the writer from all secular tasks because his work needed a frolic health to execute.

Plenipotence of health; for health was the first muse, comprising the magical effects of air, landscape and exercise upon the mind. And silence was the second. How true was Fra Angelico's remark that "he who practised the art of painting had need of quiet, and should live without cares and anxious thoughts"! How like his own the experience of that old Chinese painter who wrote: "Unless I dwell in a quiet house, seat myself in a retired room, with the windows open, the table dusted, incense burning, and ten thousand trivial thoughts crushed out and sunk, I cannot have good feeling for painting or beautiful taste, and cannot create the Yu." Proclus was right. "How can the soul be adjacent to the One, except by laying asleep the garrulous matter that is in her?"

His own primal rule was to defend the morning, to keep all its dews on, to relieve it with fine foresight from any jangle of affairs. A stroll in the orchard first, in spring and summer, attuned him for the day. But he knew many other stimulants, many other provocative influences. Ben Jonson, Shakespeare, Fletcher smote and aroused him. He sat there, torpid as a clod, and suddenly at a phrase the rigid fibres relaxed and his whole frame expanded to the welcome heats; life returned to a finger, a hand, a foot; he felt as it were wings unfolding at his side, and he saw his right to the heavens and the farthest fields of the earth. He had been but a moment before as a ship aground, and the waters returned beneath him, and he put forth his sails and turned his head to the sea. A Greek epigram sometimes turned the tide, a verse of Herrick, a page from the Neo-Platonists. Nectar, opium, these latter, as he let sail before him the pleasing and grand images of the gods and the demoniacal men of Proclus. He heard of rumors rife among the azonic gods, of demons with fulgid eyes, of the unenvying and exuberant will of the gods, of the aquatic gods and the Plain of Truth, the meadow, the paternal port. What pictorial distinctness!—as if the gods were present. "This is that which emits the intelligible light that, when it appeared, astonished the intellectual gods and made them admire their father, as Orpheus says. "What rhetoric!" These rare, brave words filled him with hilarity and spring. His heart danced, his sight was quickened, he beheld shining relations between all things. He was impelled to write, he was almost impelled to sing.

No need to tell this man the secret that beside the energy of his conscious intellect he was capable of new energy by abandonment to the nature of things. The perfection of writing was when the animal thought, and a little wine and good food furnished some elemental wisdom, and the fire too as it burned on a winter's day; for he fancied that his logs, which had grown so long in the sun and wind at Walden, were a kind of muses. Why should one spare any stimulant, any purgative, that brought one into a productive state, to the top of one's condition? How easily, alas, one lapsed into flesh and sleep!

Health, south wind, books, old trees, a boat, a friend—auspicious all; and the fair water that Demosthenes drank. There was inspiration for Emerson in any assertion of the will, in a glance at the first proposition of Political Economy: "Everything in the world is purchased by labor, and our passions are only causes of labor." Then walking had the best value as gymnastics: with the first step over the threshold of his study he would suddenly get a fresh perception of his subject more just and searching than hours of toil had given him. The sight of a man of genius filled him with a boundless confidence in his own powers; and certain trifling expedients sometimes served. Writing letters, for instance. When thoughts refused to come and the gift of the happy phrase, the bright image, seemed to have vanished forever, he would begin to write to some friend, and behold, there he was, floating off on the most cordial tide of expression. And the power of the fetish was not to be despised. Handel always composed in court dress, and Machiavelli, before sitting down at his writing-table in the evening, threw off the garments of the day and arrayed himself in his robe of ceremony. Was there not some virtue in this association? Some virtue in his own coat, made for him in Florence, which he wore when he wrote his essay on Michaelangelo?

As a final stratagem, for perfect seclusion, he would go to a hotel: in summer, some country inn, in winter the American House in Hanover Street. Even in Concord, even on his little farm, there were always distractions, running feet in the halls, a leak in the roof, a disaster in the garden. The day was cut up into short strips, and the world seemed to be in a conspiracy to invade him, to vanquish him with details, to break him into crumbs and fritter his time. Friend, wife, child, fear, want, charity, all knocked at his door at the critical moment, rang larums in his ear, scared away the muse and spoiled the poem. (And the carpenters, the masons, the tradesmen. Did they think a writer was an idler because he worked with invisible tools, worked to invisible ends?) Then a few days in Boston, at Nantasket Beach, in the mountains, made all the difference. No distractions there, no visitors. Not an insect's hum to shake the quiet hours.

The moment of inspiration—he was its reverent slave. He watched and hailed its aurora from afar.

V

LECTURING

A DUBIOUS business, lecturing. He felt as one turned out of doors, living on a balcony, living on the street. A profanation too, these Peter Parley's stories of Uncle Plato, these puppet-shows of the Eleusinian mysteries. But his debts were piling up: he had to make the plunge into this odious river of travellers, these wild eddies of hotels and boarding-houses, these dangerous precincts of charlatanism, that out of all the evil he might draw a little good.

Travelling was very instructive, if only its lessons were more immediately applicable! He could not use them all in seven transmigrations of Indur—hardly one of them in this present mortal and visible. On the road he had no thoughts, no aims, and seemed never to have had any; and he met too many people. It was all very well for Napoleonic temperaments, impassive, unimpressible by others. He was not himself a pith-ball or raw silk, yet nothing could have been stranger than the way in which people acted on him: their mere presence turned him to wood and to stone. If he talked with a man of sense and kindness he was imparadised at once, but the powerful, practical type disconcerted him and made him less than he was. He was forced to live in the country, if only because the streets made him desolate.

Strange how long one's novitiate lasted! As long as one continued to grow and did not inveterate, one was subject to circumstances and never quite controlled them. All the chemical agents acted with force on Emerson, and he came, as he felt, a greenhorn to every conversation. The young, the knowing, the fashionable, the political, the Pharisee and the Sadducee were able to strike him dumb: to human electricity no man was more susceptible. Hypersensitive hermit that he was, so much the more need for him to get an occasional shock, to run out into new places and multiply his chances for observation.

To the road, the Lyceum again! He had no alternative. So off he went, whisked away by the stormy wing of Fate and whirled like a dry leaf across the continent.

It was none too pleasant, this junketing, this wading, riding, running and suffering all manner of bumps and bruises. None too pleasant, for a decorous New Englander, dragged out of house and position for this juvenile career, carted about the country at the tail of a discourse, to read it over and over. (Sleeping in railroad stations and hotels where the very air was buttered and the whole atmosphere a volatilized beefsteak.) None too pleasant, for the "Celebrated Metaphysician," as one of the papers called him, this tumbling about in close, dirty cars, this getting to bed at midnight in a freezing room, getting up at five and breakfasting off half-washed crockery, on cold fried fish and potatoes swimming in fat.... "I'll bet you fifty dollars a day you will never leave your library and put up with all these miseries!" ... "I'll bet I will, and win the $900!"

A ridiculous vice of men, Emerson said to himself, forever consulting their dignity! They couldn't go into the quarrel, they couldn't go into the tavern, because they were old; or into the Abolition meeting and attempt to make a speech—it would never do if they failed! For himself, he looked at the wise and saw he was very young; he looked at the stars, he thought of the myriads of aspirant souls, and he saw he was a stranger and a youth and had yet his spurs to win. Absurd, these airs of age! *Ancora imparo.* He carried his satchel still.

Like a poet, yes—no dainty, protected person, apart and odd. A traveller on the common highway, a frequenter of taverns, very naturally and heartily there. A student of botany who had learned that a tree draws only one-twentieth of its nourishment from the ground, that it drinks in the rest through its leaves from the outer air. A merchant of the simples and herbs of wisdom, of the laws of Plato and Buddha, who had found that if he mixed them with a little Boston water he could sell them in New York and Ohio. An economist who had discovered that the more he spent the more he had to spend, that when he communicated all the results of his thinking he was full of new thoughts. He raked the bright atoms of perception faster together by quitting his fireside and sallying out in pursuit of them. Besides, it was always an incentive to be obliged to prove his quality all over again with every stranger he met.

He learned the resources of the country. He encountered the revolutionary force in the most unlikely corners. Very young in their education were those who required distinguished men in order to see grand traits: he found them in porters and sweeps. All sorts of surprising souls turned up at his lectures: that poor Platonist Taylor, for instance, at Amesbury, and the shoemaker at Berwick, Maine, and Tufts at Lima, New York. And Thomas Truesdale, the Wall Street cotton-broker, and Rebecca Black, the seamstress, Hermann who made the toys and Edward Stubler, the druggist in Alexandria. What natural clearness of insight these people had and how they confirmed his faith in human nature! It was true that man was an angel in disguise, a god playing the fool, that he wanted to be awakened, to get his soul out of bed, to be stirred from his deep habitual sleep to a sense of his own power to shake the world. He wanted to be awakened, that prosy, selfish sensualist, and who was able to do it better than Emerson himself? As a magnet separates the particles of steel in a heap of filings and rubbish, so in the minds of his listeners he separated all that was active, creative and fine from the slothful remainder. Life, at the sound of his voice, sprang out of apathy, and faith out of unbelief.

Who could resist that voice, with its wild, strange melody, with its intonations and cadences as of some Hungarian dance? Or that speaker, motionless on the platform, save for an occasional thrust of his right hand, clenched with the fingers upward? (Straight and thin as a birch-tree in winter, with his hatchet face, half Indian, half the face of a sagacious, peering eagle.) His voice, one listener observed, seemed to have no connection with the physical man. It had shoulders in it which he had not, lungs far larger than his, a walk the public never saw, a fist which his own hand never gave him the model for. It was as if the heavy and vase-like blossom of a magnolia, with fragrance enough to perfume a whole wilderness, had been dropped by the wind into the branch of an aspen.

He was on his way to Maine. Many and many a mile, through wastes of snow and pine-trees, the villages few and cold as Tobolsk in Siberia; and, staring into the white night, he dreamed he had committed some crime against the Czar and was bound a thousand versts into arctic Asia. But Maine was a great country: he looked at the merchants in the car—independent, with sufficient manners and more manly force of all kinds than most of the scholars he had known. (A pity, but why deny it?) These Yankees were people who, if they once got hold of a rope's end or a spar, would make it carry them; if they could but find so much as a stump or a log, they would whittle out of it a house and a barn, a farm and stock, a mill and a village, a railroad and a bank. What enemies of labor, and therefore friends of man, making wind and tide, waterfall, cloud and lightning do the work, by every art and device their cunningest brains could achieve! And here they were beside him, bound for Bangor. (And sneering a little at Maine, like all the Boston merchants. They said they could buy the State and have eighty millions left. But they didn't seem to consider that the values of Boston were artificial values, the value of luxuries, furniture, inflated prices of land and house-lots and houses, whilst the values of Maine were primary and necessary and therefore permanent under any state of society.)

But what had all these things to do with literature? He thought of his aesthetic friends, with their pale, sickly, etiolated indoor minds. Writers, he said to himself, must honor the people's facts. (Shakespeare did, or they would not be discussing him now.) If they had no place for the people, the people would have none for them; and, whatever they had to say or do, if to them politics was nothing, navigation nothing, railroads nothing, men and women nothing, they might have their seat or sphere in another planet, but never in this. The earth and sea and air, the constitution of things, and all that men call Fate, were on the people's side; and fate was a reasoner not liable to a fallacy.

Bangor! There was the committee of local magnates waiting at the station to escort him to his lodging. The owner of the best house had carried off the prize, but the whole town had been talking about him, around the stoves in the stores and over the fences. At home he was only known in connection with the cows and his name was *moo;* but he was a great man in Bangor. And in York and Paris and Bath. And what amusing characters he met on the road! The worthy W. W., for instance, who remarked, "Three things make the gentleman, the hat, the collar and the boots." (Ah, that Professor Teufelsdröckh had heard the word!) And the man in the coach with his contrivance for defending his coffin in the grave from body-snatchers. He had devised a pistol to go off—*pop!*—from this end, and a pistol—*pop!*—from that end of the coffin; and he was plainly spending his life in the sweets of that posthumous revenge.

There were journeys to foreign lands, Philadelphia, Baltimore; for Emerson's fame was spreading, and they wanted to hear him in those regions too. Cosy rides in the cabin of the Jersey ferry-boat, where he found himself snugly ensconced in the warm entrails of an argument with a Presbyterian clergyman. Bear's meat like this was not to be had at home: he might have been in Scotland again with all this Princeton brimstone. (But how these sects fattened on each other's faults! How many men got a living by calling the Unitarians prayerless, or by showing that the Calvinists were bigots, while the poor devil who only saw faults in himself died in his sins.) The Catholic Cathedral in Baltimore was a great relief, with the pictures, the lighted altar, the swinging censer, with every whiff bringing all Rome again to Emerson's mind. How dignified, this shrine, where priest and people were nothing and for once an idea excluded these impertinences! He detested, for an hour, the Reformation and the Parliament of Barebones, the Protestant with his "private judgment" and his family pews and doctrinaires and schismatics. The Catholic Church, he felt, was the church of poets; it ignored the private man, it respected masses and ages, it was in harmony with Nature which loved the race and cared nothing for the individual. Well he could understand the joyful adhesion of the Winckelmanns and the Schlegels—just as one seizes with delight the fine romance and tosses the learned Heeren out of the window. (Unhappily with the sigh that follows the romance—"Ah, that one word of it were true!")

The Philadelphians "listened with great pleasure to the chaste and beautiful lecture of the Boston essayist." (Or so the newspaper said.) A dull, timorous town, he thought, with a very lymphatic appearance; and he looked eagerly for the stars at night, for fear they should disappear in the torpid air.

New York was an outpost of home, for his brother William was living on Staten Island. He had settled at Dutch Farms (he had christened the village Concord), as judge of Richmond County. William was no longer the isolated man that Emerson used to fancy him; he seemed to be an important part of the web of life on the island, as genial as possible now, riding down to Richmond in his gig or strolling along the road with his dogs: good company, in his Snuggery (as one couldn't but call the house), or out for a ramble on Todt Hill, where Emerson stopped for a moment to cut a walking-stick. Henry Thoreau had come down to tutor his son; but Henry was unhappy. (Was there too much starch in the Judge's house?) A pity, really; Henry was a little narrow. Why should he despise everything outside of Concord?

Henry was very droll (with the mud of the

Concord River still on his boots) discussing New York, the Academy exhibition, the "Great Western," the sidewalks ("no give to the foot"), the cabmen at the ferry ("Want a cab, sir? Want a *nice* cab, sir?"—"A sad sight," said Henry), the churches these people bragged about, the pigs in the streets ("the most respectable part of the population"), the immigrant laborers hustling off the ships, the English travellers on their way to the Astor House, to whom he had "done the honors of the city" ("mere herds of men," said Henry)—the whole town meaner and more pretentious even than Boston. But he liked the hum (from a distance) and the roar of the sea; and he had found a few things on Staten Island that were worth a little attention. The sunsets were not bad, and they had a fine red honeysuckle there that ought to be transplanted to Concord, and he had heard of a certain tulip-tree—but of this he had some doubts. Homesick Henry! He could not have been more disgruntled.

But Henry was not so wrong when he talked of the editors and the magazines, Mr. Willis' *New Mirror* and the *Ladies' Companion*. ("I couldn't write anything companionable," said Henry.) He needed the money badly, and he had rambled, he said, into every bookseller's and publisher's house in the city; and he found that he talked with these poor men as if he were over head and ears in business. But they proposed to him to do, as he put it, what an honest man could not—a "very valuable experience," said Henry. Let them stick to New York and the West for their contributions. One had other things on one's mind in Massachusetts.

So Henry went back to the Judge's house. "Literature" was not for him. He spent his evenings translating the "Seven Against Thebes" and looking into Pindar. But he had heard, seen or met the most interesting people in New York. He had called upon Horace Greeley, the latter-day Franklin, who had just started the *Tribune* ("Now be neighborly," said Horace), and William Henry Channing, who had started a magazine himself, called *The Present* (and was "sadly in earnest," as Henry remarked, "discussing the question, What to do for the race?"), and Lucretia Mott, the Quaker preacher in Hester Street. (What poise that woman had, in the hurly-burly of the anti-Abolition mob! "Tar and feathers? Go ahead, my dears!") But the best friend he had made was Henry James, the "little, fat, rosy Swedenborgian amateur," as Ellery Channing called him, "with the look of a broker and the brains and heart of a Pascal."

EMERSON AND OTHERS

A sterling man, this James, said Concord Henry, so patient and so determined to have the good of you. He humanized New York.

Henry had missed nothing but the inessentials. (He had even talked with young Albert Brisbane, who had just come home from Paris and had taken a daily column in the *Tribune* to explain the doctrines of Fourier.) But for Emerson the inessentials had their charm. These crowds of passers-by—a lovely child, a heroic-looking man: could he only have stopped and told them how much they attracted him! There was Barnum's Museum too. (The sea-serpent had an instinct to retire into the depths of the sea when about to die. He was sadly afraid of the naturalists, but his heart sank within him when he heard that Barnum was born.) Captain Rynders, the Tammany boss, was well worth a glance: a blackguard, of course, but almost a consolation among so many palefaces. And then there was always fashion in New York. Milliners with a skill and French with an accent that one never found in Boston.

Trifles, no doubt, and not for Henry. But Bryant was no trifle. A "true bard, but simple," a tyrant over the young. People talked of the clever shopmen who advertised their wares on the Palisades and the rocks by the railroad: this man, more cunning by far, had contrived to levy on all American Nature. Not a waterfall, not a gentian but Bryant had bribed to speak for him. What usurpation was this?—that who spoke of the autumn woods, of the gardens of the desert, of any feature of day or night in the country, was forced to remember Bryant. But he talked like a man whose great days were over when Emerson called to see him in his office at the *Evening Post*. He was free from all pretension, direct, plain-spoken, but suffering manifestly from want of culture, with no time for himself, no time for books or thoughts (weltering all day long in a foam of papers). He stared and rubbed his eyes when Emerson spoke of his poetry—said all such things were for boys and girls and the aged, that men in middle life had too much else to think of. And then he gave such a look—

"Now my weary lips I close,
Leave me, leave me to repose."

But Horace Greeley, of course, was the great New Yorker. He was always following somebody, and everyone followed him. He was following Doctor Graham at the moment, the high priest of brown-bread: after bolting his food for thirty years, ransacking the table with his long arms, as if Time's chariot were after him, he had made up his mind—in silence and the tears of indigestion—that the gospel of "little meat" had much to be said for it. He was living in a Graham boarding-house when Emerson went to find him, and he dashed in with his coat-tails on the wind. (A sunny soul, this Greeley, with his round, honest face, like a ripe New Hampshire pumpkin! With the wrinkles in his coat, with the necktie under his ear, with his stockings round his ankles and his great ploughman's boots. And with Brisbane at his heels.) Bang went the beaver on the rack. "Here's Brisbane," said Horace. "He wanted to meet you." And they all fell to. (Our Horace did. What manners! "Will you have a little salad, Mr. Greeley?"— "You can be fixing me some.")

So this was "neighborly" Horace, still reaching for the butter, with his pockets bulging with seeds (and papers and pamphlets). Could anything have been more encouraging in a Whiggish age than a farmer's boy in the city of New York, adopting every benevolent crotchet and maintaining it, and making the people sit up! Carlyle was right again: "The journalists are now the true kings and clergy." And Emerson could only wish long life to the *Tribune*, long life and a million readers.

EMERSON: SIX EPISODES

Brisbane was eloquent too, when Emerson saw him again, at the Globe Hotel. He wanted Emerson to join him—"come in," with all his "party," for he evidently thought of the Boston Transcendentalists as a sort of phalanx, much like Fourier's own. And what pictures he drew of the world when the Fourierists had straightened it out! What palaces, what concerts for all! What lectures and poetry and flowers! What perfections of tillage and architecture, gardens and baths! They were going to cover the planet with "groups" and communities. And all the poets and artists and Transcendental persons were to flock to Constantinople—(they were far too great for their Concords, New Yorks and Bostons)—for music, society and wit such as words could never describe.

It was very attractive indeed, this Attractive Industry, though Emerson thought he could mention a few real mischiefs—living for show, losing the whole in the particular, indigence of vital power—that would appear as much in a phalanstery as in a tub. And it figured man as a thing, a thing to be ripened or retarded, moulded or polished, turned into fluid or gas at the will of the leader. It was rather embarrassing for Emerson: Brisbane had misconceived him, misread his political theories—had not seen that he was a poet, of no more use in such a scheme than a rainbow or a firefly. He had to make endless disclaimers and explanations: "I am not at all the sort of man you supposed." (For Brisbane was painfully literal. He spoke of Transcendentalism as a known and fixed element, like salt or meal.) But how cheering, in spite of all, he felt, as he left the hotel, how cheering in a day of small and fierce undertakings, were projects of such friendly aims and such bold and generous proportions!

He was travelling westward now, each year farther and farther. St. Louis, Springfield, Milwaukee. He was going to school to the prairies, where it rained and thawed incessantly and he stepped off the new-paved streets and was up to his shoulders in mud. Well he knew the bitter evenings, the "singers" of Illinois, when the mercury stood at 28° below zero and the landlord merrily said they had no cold weather in those regions, only Indian summer occasionally and coolish nights. He slept on the floor of canal-boats, wrapped in a buffalo-robe, in a wreath of legs, and drove in buggies across the plains fifty miles in the icy wind. And many a time he saw the waves of Lake Michigan tossing in a bleak snowstorm.

The world out there, as the settler said, was

"done up in larger lots." The talk was all of sections and quarter-sections (of swamp and forest); there were placards in the hotels pleading against the fury of expectoration and saying that no gentleman could come to the public table without his coat; and he didn't need to discover that in all he called cultivation these kindly, sinewy farmers were only ten years old. How could he be surprised when the stout Illinoisan, after giving him a ten-minutes' trial, stamped out of the hall? He was more the student than the teacher in this land of wonders, where the prairie grass at La Salle was higher than the top of his carriage, higher than the head of a man riding on horseback. He had always delighted in men who could "do" things, men of the drastic class, and the Western farmers had drawn from their local necessities what stores of heroic energy! They lived on venison and quails like children of Homer.

He encountered again those men who were natural founders of cities, kings of Norway, sensible, steady, wise and prompt in action. And towns and towns, solid and stately squares turned out as if by machinery, like cloth and hardware. And countless other marvels, inanimate marvels, unfused as yet with the electric will of man. Interminable silent forests, the raw bullion of Nature. Miles of acres at Pittsburgh, each with three or four bottoms, rich soil, bituminous coal, iron, salt (almost as many bottoms as the soul of man). And the Mammoth Cave in Kentucky, where he lost the light of a day, where he walked under mimic stars and sailed on Stygian streams, eighteen miles in the darkness. And relics of a fathomless past. A mass of copper, unearthed near Lake Superior (six tons? or twenty-three?), standing on end, on wedges, with a wooden bowl beside it, and axes and chisels of stone. And what strange confirmations of his reading! He happened to be glancing through Tacitus, *"De Germanis,"* in Missouri and Illinois, and he noted all sorts of resemblances between the Germans of the Hercynian forest and these Hoosiers, Suckers and Badgers of the American woods.

He always enjoyed his adventures in Horace Greeley's country. (For Horace was the spiritual father of all these regions. What bales of *Tribunes* were dispersed there every day! Horace did everyone's thinking for two dollars a year.) He liked to get away from the Eastern sea-board, from Boston, Cambridge, New York, where the current of American life was so superficial. The nervous, rocky West was intruding a new and continental element into the national mind: out there the passion for Europe had yielded to the passion for America and he seemed to discern the dawn of a native genius. How good it was, this vast sloven continent, with its high Alleghany pastures and the sea-wide, sea-skirted prairie where slept and murmured still the great mother Nature! Still asleep, Nature, though almost conscious, too much by half for man. A little *triste,* perhaps, with all this rank vegetation of swamps and forests, steeped in dews and rains. But what a poem!

VI

IN CONCORD

SUMMER days had come to Concord, those glowing summer days that made him sad because he could only spend them once. He sighed for the thousand heads and thousand bodies of the Indian gods, that he might celebrate this immense beauty in many ways and places.

These were the days for walks, the little walks and the long walks: a dash to the top of the ridge across the road where he saw Wachusett and Monadnock on the shimmering horizon, or a stroll to the Estabrook region, with its old straggling orchards and clearings and cellar-holes, seventeenth century farms, abandoned for generations, lapsing back into forest. (Where apples grew in autumn that were never found in the market, the "Beware-of-this," the "Bite-me-if-you-dare," apples bursting with cider.) Or the shorter walks in the wild garden at

Walden. For Emerson had bought a woodlot, a wild rocky ledge along the pond, with a populous grove of chestnuts, oaks and hemlocks sweeping down to the shore. Some of the trees were old but an undergrowth of maples, pines and birches had sprung up to the water's edge. At first he had spent whole days there, with pruning-shears and hatchet, cutting paths and opening vistas. And there, above all, he loved to stroll and linger, bathing, reading on the bank, jotting in his notebooks.

Hours like these were as centuries, loaded, fragment. His spirits rose as he closed his gate behind him, and the moment he entered the pastures he found antiquity again. In the fields with the lowing cattle, the birds, the bees, the waters, the satisfying outlines of the landscape, he could not have said whether it was Tempe, Thessaly, Enna or familiar Concord. A mile to the pond, now by the road, now by the gulley along the track, and books, affairs, petulance and fret were forgotten. Every bird, every plant, every spring, every light from the sky, every shadow on the earth detained him as he wandered hither and thither.

What health, what affinity he found there! Before him was the pond itself, blue and beautiful in the bosom of the woods and under the amber sky, like a sapphire lying in the moss. Overhead floated the summer clouds, here soft and feathery, there firm and continental, vanishing in the East into plumes and auroral gleams, with an expression of immense amplitude in their dotted and rippled rack. No crowding in that upper air, but a boundless cheerfulness and strength: how they seemed to enjoy, those clouds, their height and privilege of motion! The chickadees, the robins, the bluebirds, perching on the iron arms of the oaks, the chestnut trees with their towers of white blossoms, even the waterflies on the pond were full of happiness. The very look of the woods was heroic and stimulating, and trees, birds, clouds and insects seemed parts of the eternal chain of destiny.

A symphony indeed for a man with musical eyes. Emerson had often regretted that he had no ear, but what others heard, as it seemed to him, he saw. All the soothing, brisk or romantic moods that corresponding melodies awakened in them, he found in the carpet of the wood, in the margin of the pond, in the shade of the hemlock grove or in the infinite variety and rapid dance of the treetops. The thrilling leap of the squirrel up the long bough of pine, the stems of oak and chestnut gleaming like steel on the excited eye, the floating, exhaling, evanescent beauty of the summer air were enchantment enough for him. The names of the reeds and the grasses were a lively pleasure, the milkweeds and the gentians, the mallows, the nymphaea, the cardinal-flower, the button-bush, the willow with its green smoke. What poems these names often were: Erigeron, the Old Man of the Spring, so called because it grows too early, the Chimaphila, Lover of Winter, the Plantain, called by the Indians the White Man's Foot because it follows man wherever he builds a hut. And the odorous waving of the flowers charmed him. It was like returning to some ancestral home to rejoin these vegetable demons: his heart seemed to pump through his body the sap of this forest of verdure. He ceased to be a person; he was conscious of the blood of thousands coursing through him. As he opened with his fingers the buds of the birch and the oak, as his eyes followed the thistle-balls drifting in space, covered with their bright races, each particle a counterpart and contemplator of the whole, he felt himself dilating and conspiring with the summer breeze.

Was there ever a more abandoned lotus-eater? But was it not for this idleness that all his affairs existed? Why should he hurry homeward? Allah never counted the time the Arab spent in the chase! Had he not come back to his own, made friends with the elements?—and why should he part with them now? The mind loved its old home, and he tasted every moment; the active magic reached his dust; he expanded in the warm day like corn and melons. Lying there on the bare ground with his head bathed by the blithe air, he was happy in his universal relations. The name of his nearest friend sounded foreign and accidental; he was the heir of uncontained beauty and power. He hesitated to move a finger, to lift his book, lest he should disturb the sweet vision.

He felt as if he had drunk the soma-juice with the morning-moving deities of the Rig-Veda, as if life were all an eternal resource and a long tomorrow, rich and strong as yesterday. Goethe had known this mood: "When the healthy nature of man works in its entirety, when he feels himself in the world as in a large, beautiful, worthy and solid whole, when his harmonious well-being assures him a clear, free joy, then would the universe, if it were conscious, exult as arrived at its aim and admire the summit of its own being and becoming." And there were other times and other spots—how many! —autumn, winter, night, the river. Those Indian summer days, for instance, when heaven and earth glowed with magnificence and he could almost see the Indians under the trees in the wood, when Florida and Cuba seemed to have left their seats and come to Concord, when all the insects were out and the birds came forth, when the cattle lying on the ground seemed to have great thoughts and India and Egypt looked through their eyes. Winter days, when the leafless trees became spires of flame in the sunset, and the stars of the dead chalices of the flowers and every withered stem and bit of stubble rimed with frost contributed to the mute music. Winter evenings, when from every gray or slate-colored cloud over the whole dome depended a wreath of roses, and the long slender bars swam like fishes in the sea of crimson light, and the stars emerged with their private, ineffable glances. And days and nights of paddling up the river. What colors were in the water then, as the paddle stirred it, the hue of Rhine wine, jasper and verd antique, gold and green and chestnut and hazel; and what sorcery as he returned in the evening when the moon was making amber of the world, when every cottage pane glittered with silver, and the little harlot flies of the lowlands sparkled in the grass, and the meadows sent up the rank smells of all their ferns and folded flowers into a nocturnal fragrance. Summer nights on the moving water, summer noons at Walden! Everything invited him to repose, to the dreams of the Oriental sages.

Yes, he was "adjacent to the One" at such moments as these. Moments, hours of perception, when the solitude of the body was the populousness of the soul, when he felt himself in active touch with that force, known of old to the Buddhists, which sleeps in plants, awakens in animals and becomes conscious in man. His mind became rampant as the tropical growth; he melted into the earth and felt all its organs at work within him. He had left his human relations far behind him, wife, child, friends, and returned to matter, to the rocks, to the ground, and he seemed of one substance with air, light, carbon, lime and granite. He became a moist, cold element. Frogs piped, waters far off tinkled, dry leaves hissed, grass bent and rustled, and he had died out of the world of men and come to feel a strange aqueous, terraqueous, aerial, etherial sympathy and existence. . . . The trance of how many sages!—gymnosophists reclining on their flowery banks, hermits of Ceylon, Chinese philosophers in bamboo groves, charmed by the plashing of bright cascades. . . . A swoon, an awakening;

for, coming back to himself, he seemed to have traversed all the cycles of life. How truly Pythagoras had expressed it!—"One mind runs through the universe." And that other saying of the Greeks: "The soul is absorbed into God as a phial of water broken in the sea."

JOHN BUTLER YEATS

JOHN BUTLER YEATS

My memory of John Butler Yeats goes back to 1908, to a little gas-lit bedroom in the old Grand Union Hotel, whither I had been taken to meet the "father of the poet." At that time the Irish Literary Revival was at its height, and there were no names more glamorous than Yeats and Synge. The "father of the poet," with his air of a benevolent sage, looked the part to perfection, looked it and spoke it indeed so perfectly that he shone at first only with innumerable reflected lights. He had come to America for a fortnight; he was to stay for thirteen years. He was to experience between the ages of sixty-nine and eighty-three a second career as affluent as his first had been. How soon it was to be forgotten that he was any one's father! In that early time —it was natural enough—he pulled for us at all the strings of association. If he had not seen Shelley plain, he had been as an art-student a commensal of Samuel Butler and William Morris; he had been one of the first Whitmanians —Whitman sent him his "affectionate remembrance" in a letter of 1872; for forty years he had agreed with York Powell and disagreed with Edward Dowden; he had known the father of Wilde and the mother of Shaw. All these recollections he poured out in a stream of enchanting anecdotes. He was lost for us at first in the light of his own talk.

His earlier career, to be sure, had been wanting in no element of the illuminative, when it was not the paradoxical. It was the career, as rumor told us, of genius in solution, or at least not too forbiddingly crystallized, the career of being human to such a tune that two generations of Irish poets and artists had grown up literally under its wing. The story of Mr. Yeats' Dublin studio is to be found in Miss Katharine Tynan's autobiography and I do not know how many other books, just as the record of his influence is to be found in his elder son's "Reveries over Childhood and Youth." Never, surely, had a man been more the cause of a more various wit in others, and this without prejudice to his having been—shall I say?—the Reynolds of a stirring age in his nation's history. He had painted all the distinguished, the interesting, the charming men and women of his time, painted them with such insight and such grace that his gathered work constitutes of itself—remote as it must have been from any suggestion of the public, the official—a sort of National Portrait Gallery. He would not paint the dull, if only, it might seem, because it was they who wished to pay him for the trouble: it was the angel of impecuniosity, I remember his remarking, that had given him his freedom, a sensitive angel, no doubt, whose protection he wished not to jeopardize. His studio was thus closed only to clients—he would fly to escape from a lucrative commission, which meant that there would not be good talk during the sittings, the good talk that implied a current of sympathy. Nor was this merely petulant: he could paint only those whom he saw, and he could see only those whom he admired. He painted, as Swinburne criticized, for the "noble pleasure of praising." In this, as in so many other respects, his fashion was that of the ancients; and one cannot but think that his pride, and all this multiform expression of his pride, must have had its effect in the rebirth of the Irish spirit.

Such questions could hardly have interested Mr. Yeats himself. "Your artist and poet, unless he becomes a rhetorician," he wrote in one of his last essays, "is a solitary and self-immersed in his own thoughts and has no desire to impress other people." It was thus that we were to see him, a true solitary himself, and never more so than when he most suggested (to those who did not know him) the autocrat of the dinner-table. But as time went on I think his interest in painting in a measure dropped away. When he first came to New York, it was still strong; in the early days at Petitpas' he always had a sketch-book in his pocket and would draw as he talked; to the end his letters, his briefest notes, were usually adorned with a little pen-and-ink impression—of himself, as a rule, and not too hasty to fix some humorous or ironic "state of the soul." I imagine, however, that few of the portraits he did here were as good as those he had done at home, perhaps because his sitters were not initiated into the secret, which must have been legendary in Dublin, that unless his pictures were carried off, tactfully but forcibly, at the right moment, he was sure to overpaint and spoil them. His son speaks of his having painted a pond somewhere in Ireland: "He began it in spring and painted all through the year, the picture changing with the seasons, and gave it up unfinished when he had painted the snow upon the heath-covered banks." Everyone discovered this trait sooner or later, but in New York it was usually later: it was not the open secret it might have been if his American sitters had been able to compare notes. And besides, who could escape from his presence?—like Socrates, he was a flute-player more wonderful than Marsyas, who charmed us with the voice only. His art suffered in consequence, for he required the co-operation of a practical and resolute sitter. Alas, he should have painted only men without ears.

It was at Petitpas' that his star rose for us. He had found his way to that friendly house within a year of his arrival and was not to leave it again; and there he had his "Indian summer of the mind," a Jovian old age without any visible counterpart in a country where age as well as youth obeys the counsel of Mr. Rockefeller—not to talk but to saw wood. For his play of conversation he required no such preliminaries as Sarah Battle—there was no rigor in Mr. Yeats' game; yet one condition he would not forego—a clear, abundant light. He disliked the duplicity of the candle-lit American interior; he wished to follow the expressions of his interlocutors and would recall the luminous mahogany tables of old that reflected the dazzling chandelier and brightened the faces from below as they were brightened from above. The lights were high in Twenty-ninth Street—witness John Sloan's portrait-group, "Yeats at Petitpas'," or even George Bellows' murky lithograph of the same subject. It was really characteristic, this desire, for it signified that our philosopher could not have loved art so much had he not loved human nature more.

His conversation was all of human nature. It flowed with every sort of engaging contradiction, with a wisdom that was by turns cheerful and tragic and a folly that was always somehow wise. Mr. W. B. Yeats tells us that when he was a boy his father would choose to read to him the "less abstract" poets; he preferred Keats to Shelley and the first half of "Prometheus Unbound" to the second. During the last few years the metaphysical habit grew upon him, and, as he had a terminology all his own, it was sometimes difficult to follow him. Yet even then, as he distinguished between "feeling" and "emotion," for instance, or "brains" and "intellect," one discerned his point without, so to say, perceiving it—nothing annoyed him so much as to be pressed for a definition. Besides, his point never failed to bury itself in one's mind: one would find oneself puzzling it out years afterward. He had lost some of his mischievousness, so that he would no longer maintain, for instance, that even English tailors are inferior, but he still clothed his discourse in the gayest web of images. He would say of the difference between a photograph and a portrait that the photograph is like the description of a ball given by a jaded, bored, literal-minded old chaperon, the painting like a description of the same ball given by a pretty girl who has thoroughly enjoyed herself. He would picture the Puritan minister "sitting in company with the father of the family in a sort of horrid conspiracy to poison life at its sources." He would tell of some Irish peasant who, describing a well-dressed man, added that he "fell away in the breeches." Or he would call up some picture from the past, as, for instance, of John Richard Green, in the days when he was known as a brilliant man who had done nothing and was not expected to do anything—of Green, in some drawing-room, surrounded by admirers, and remarking in a high chant: "All women seek to combine two mutually incompatible positions, the position of perfect strength and the position of perfect weakness."

He had forgotten nothing that revealed human nature at its most singular, touching, absurd, above all its most characteristic. He could forgive anything but rhetoric, legality, emotionality and gregariousness—these were his four abominations. He had had reason in his own country to deplore the folly of the oratorical mind; and regarding legality his opinion was much the same as St. Paul's, that it was the "strength of sin"—perhaps he was the more certain of this because he had begun life as a lawyer himself. As for his dislike of the emotional and the gregarious, it may have been a result of certain American experiences: I know that his opinion of Whitman changed entirely after he had lived here for a while. Having admired him for years he turned against the "emotional bard," remarking in one of his later letters, "The Sacred Nine have not heard his name even to this day." Nor was he free from reservations in regard to the Celtic Revival: I remember his horror, for instance, when a rather gushing lady accused him of having had some commerce with fairies. The truth is that he was at bottom an old-fashioned Anglo-Irish country gentleman, redolent of the classics, a sceptic of the eighteenth-century tradition, who had also drunk in his youth at the spring of "political economy" and John Stuart Mill: and upon this foundation had been superadded, to the confusion of the simple, the doctrines of Rossetti in painting, of Morris in economics and of Irish Nationalism in the political sphere. It was a combination that made for an infinite, if a somewhat bewildering, wit—a wit, moreover, that drew the line on the other side of the banshee.

"Idleness and conversation" was his only formula for the good life. Like the "Be hard!" or the "Carefully cultivate your faults" of other sages, it was a stumbling-block to the foolish, among whom Mr. Yeats counted the population of Belfast and those who have "leather" faces and pursue the dollar. In his own case it signified an activity of the mind and the feelings that knew no check: for if his painting had lapsed, he wrote his first play at seventy-eight and was experimenting in poetry to the last week of his life. His "high-bred amicability," to quote Goethe's phrase about Molière, was a veritable school of manners, of the natural in manners; and he was always quick to draw out the least articulate of his companions. How many must have blessed him who had never known, until they talked with him, that they too had something to say! But what seems most fortunate now is that his exile turned him more and more to writing—his three books were all written in America. For years he had been urged to write his reminiscences—York Powell, as one discovers in the latter's correspondence, suggested it a generation ago; and his "Recollections of Samuel Butler" shows us what the book would have been. But what does it matter? He drew his own portrait in every line he wrote. Had the *Pensées* of Pascal taken their final shape we should have had only the same Pascal, plus the mortar of "rhetoric": and it is all the more characteristic that in Mr. Yeats' record we should miss the connecting links he so cheerfully ignored in life.

From his essays and his letters the thought drifts up, as Mr. Ezra Pound says, "as easily as a cloud in the heavens, and as clear-cut as clouds on bright days." In the essays his conversation lives again; in the letters we find it recollected, as it were, in tranquillity, soberer than his wont was, if only because more studied. Yet everywhere the effect is of a pure spontaneity. He will mention "the most deliciously uninteresting young girl I ever met, her perfect aplomb in selfishness was a perpetual surprise and pleasure." He will say that a "perfectly disinterested, an absolutely unselfish love of making mischief, mischief for its own dear sake, is an Irish characteristic." He will speak in this fashion of the "dungeon of self-hatred which is Puritanism":

JOHN BUTLER YEATS

The supremacy of the will power implies the malediction of human nature that has cursed English life and English letters. I referred to Bunyan as foremost in the Malediction movement. He would have called Hamlet "Mr. Facing Both-Ways," and Juliet "Miss Bold Face" or "Carnality," and Romeo "Mr. Lovelorn," and Macbeth "Mr. Henpecked," etc., finding where he could epithets and names to belittle and degrade the temple of human nature and all its altars.

He will press to the depths and return with this:

"Except for one or two I have never had a happy day," said the magnificently fortunate Goethe. The never-dying aches of the probe of pain are in every bosom: only while others resort to some kind of laudanum the poets let these work, finding in them the root of happiness, the only sort which, though it be twin with sorrow, is without a fleck on its purity.

He will recur to those leading ideas—that "desire and not emotion is the substance of art," that "character is the self-evolved enemy of personality," that "in obeying rules, the highest even, we shall never forget that in so doing we are not alive"—which underlay all his other thoughts and expressed his own "certitude of belief." His mind was of such a perfect candor that the printed page reproduces it like a sensitive plate; we hear him talking as we read, we see him stoop and smile.

No doubt the novelty of his American experience, the sharp contrast with everything he had previously known, led him thus to define his point of view. His essays on "The Modern Woman" and "Back to the Home" are markedly the fruit of such a reaction: in the presence of our chaos the disparate elements in his own mind, in his life, in his memory, flew together and he rose above them in harmonious flight. So we may say that America had its share in the making of him. It was his energy, he said, a month before he died, that kept him in his adventurous exile; but he also stayed because he liked us. That was a great compliment, and one we shall not forget.

RANDOLPH BOURNE

RANDOLPH BOURNE

RANDOLPH BOURNE was born in Bloomfield, New Jersey, May 30, 1886. He died in New York, December 22, 1918. Between these two dates was packed one of the fullest, richest and most significant lives of our generation. Its outward events can be summarized in a few words. Bourne went to the public schools in his native town, and then for some time earned his living as an assistant to a manufacturer of automatic piano music. In 1909 he entered Columbia, graduating in 1913 as holder of the Gilder Fellowship, which enabled him to spend a year of study and investigation in Europe. In 1911 he had begun contributing to *The Atlantic Monthly,* and his first book, "Youth and Life," a volume of essays, appeared in 1913. He was a member of the contributing staff of *The New Republic* during its first three years; later he was a contributing editor of *The Seven Arts* and *The Dial*. He had published, in addition to his first collection of essays and a large number of miscellaneous articles and book reviews, two other books, "Education and Living," and "The Gary Schools." At the time of his death he was engaged on a novel and a study of the political future.

It might be guessed from this that Bourne at thirty-two had not quite found himself. His interests were indeed almost universal: he had written on politics, economics, philosophy, education, literature. No other of our younger critics had cast so wide a net, and Bourne had hardly begun to draw the strings and count and sort his catch. He was a working journalist, a literary free-lance with connections often of the most precarious kind, who contrived, by daily miracles of audacity and courage, to keep himself serenely afloat in a society where his convictions prevented him from following any of the ordinary avenues of preferment and recognition. It was a feat never to be sufficiently marvelled over; it would have been striking, in our twentieth century New York, even in the case of a man who was not physically handicapped as Bourne was. But such a life is inevitably scattering, and it was only after the war had literally driven him in upon himself that he set to work at the systematic harvesting of his thoughts and experiences. He had not quite found himself, perhaps, owing to the extraordinary range of interests for which he had to find a personal common denominator; yet no other young American critic, I think, had exhibited so clear a tendency, so coherent a body of desires. His personality was not only unique, it was also absolutely expressive. I have had the delightful experience of reading through at a sitting, so to say, the whole mass of his uncollected writings, articles, essays, book reviews, unprinted fragments and a few letters, and I am astonished at the way in which, like a ball of camphor in a trunk, the pungent savor of the man spreads itself over every paragraph. Here was no anonymous reviewer, no mere brilliant satellite of the radical movement, losing himself in his immediate reactions: one finds everywhere, interwoven in the fabric of his work, the silver thread of a personal philosophy, the singing line of an intense and beautiful desire.

What was that desire? It was for a new fellowship in the youth of America as the principle of a great and revolutionary departure in our life, a league of youth, one might call it, consciously framed with the purpose of creating, out of the blind chaos of American society, a fine, free, articulate cultural order. That, as it seems to me, was the dominant theme of all his effort, the positive theme to which he always returned from his thrilling forays into the fields of education and politics, philosophy and sociology. One finds it at the beginning of his career in such essays as "Our Cultural Humility," one finds it at the end in the "History of a Literary Radical." One finds it in that pacifism which he pursued with such an obstinate and lonely courage and which was the logical outcome of the checking and thwarting of those currents of thought and feeling in which he had invested the whole passion of his life. *Place aux Jeunes* might have been his motto: he seemed indeed the flying wedge of the younger generation itself.

I shall never forget my first meeting with him, that odd little apparition with his vibrant eyes, his quick, birdlike steps and the long, black student's cape he had brought back with him from Paris. It was in November, 1914, and we never imagined then that the war was going to be more than a slash, however deep, across the face of civilization, we never imagined it was going to plough on and on until it had uprooted and turned under the soil so many green shoots of hope and desire in the young world. Bourne had published that radiant book of essays on the "Adventure of Life," the "Two Generations," the "Excitement of Friendship," with its happy and confident suggestion of the present as a sort of transparent veil hung up against the window of some dazzling future; he had had his wanderyear abroad and had come home with that indescribable air of the scholar-gypsy, his sensibility, fresh, clairvoyant, matutinal, a philosopher of the *gaya scienza,* his hammer poised over the rock of American philistinism, with never a doubt in his heart of the waters of youth imprisoned there. One divined him in a moment, the fine, mettlesome temper of his intellect, his curiosity, his acutely critical self-consciousness, his aesthetic flair, his delicate sense of personal relationships, his toughness of fibre, his masterly powers of assimilation, his grasp of reality, his burning convictions, his beautifully precise desires. Here was Emerson's American Scholar at last, but radiating an infinitely warmer, profaner, more companionable influence than Emerson had ever dreamed of, an influence that savored rather of Whitman and William James. He was the new America incarnate, with that stamp of a sort of permanent youthfulness on his queer, twisted, appealing face. You felt that in him the new America had suddenly found itself and was all astir with the excitement of its first maturity.

EMERSON AND OTHERS

His life had prepared him for the rôle, for the physical disability that had cut him off from the traditional currents and preoccupations of American life had given him a poignant insight into the predicament of all those others who, like him, could not adjust themselves to the industrial machine—the exploited, the sensitive, the aspiring, those, in short, to whom a new and very different America was no academic idea but a necessity so urgent that it had begun to be a reality. As detached as any young East Sider from the herd-unity of American life the colonial tradition, the "genteel tradition," yet passionately concerned with America, passionately caring for America, he had discovered himself at Columbia, where so many strains of the newer immigrant population meet one another in the full flood and ferment of modern ideas. He had been shut in with himself and his books, and what dreams had passed through his mind of the possibilities of life, of the range of adventures that are open to the spirit, of some great collective effort of humanity. Would there never be room for these things in America? Was it not precisely the task of the young to make room for them? Bourne's grandfather and great-grandfather had been doughty preachers and reformers: he had inherited a certain religious momentum that thrust him now into the midst of the radical tide. Above all, he had found companions who helped him to clarify his ideas and grapple with his aims. Immigrants, many of them, of the second generation, candidates for the "melting-pot" that had simply failed to melt them, they trailed with them a dozen rich, diverse racial and cultural tendencies which America seemed unable either to assimilate or to suppress. Were they not, these newcomers of the eleventh hour, as clearly entitled as the first colonials had been to a place in the sun of the great experimental democracy upon which they were making such strange new demands? They wanted a freer emotional life, a more vivid intellectual life: oddly enough, it was they and not the hereditary Americans, the "people of action," who spoke of an "American culture" and demanded it. Bourne had found his natural allies. Intensely Anglo-Saxon himself, he could not desire the triumph of the Anglo-Saxon tradition which had apparently lost itself in the pursuit of a mechanical efficiency. It was a "trans-national" America of which he caught glimpses now, a battle-ground of all the cultures, a superculture, that might perhaps, by some happy chance, determine the future of civilization itself.

EMERSON AND OTHERS

It was with some such vision as this that he had gone abroad. If that super-culture was ever to come it could only be through some prodigious spiritual organization of the youth of America, some organization that would have to begin with small and highly self-conscious groups; these groups, moreover, would have to depend for a long time upon the experience of young Europe. The very ideas of spiritual leadership, the intellectual life, the social revolution were foreign to a modern America that had submitted to the common mould of business enterprise; even philosophers like Professor Dewey had had to assume a protective coloration, and when people spoke of art they had to justify it as an "asset." For Bourne, therefore, the European tour was something more than a preparation for his own life: he was like a bird in the nesting season, gathering twigs and straw for a nest that was not to be his but young America's, a nest for which old America would have to provide the bough! He was in search, in other words, of new ideas, new attitudes, new techniques, personal and social, for which he was going to demand recognition at home, and it is this that gives to his "Impressions of Europe 1913-1914"—his report to Columbia as holder of the Gilder Fellowship—an actuality that so perfectly survives the war. Where can one find anything better in the way of social insight than his pictures of radical France, of the ferment of the young Italian soul, of the London intellectuals—Sidney Webb, lecturing "with the patient air of a man expounding arithmetic to backward children," Shaw, "clean, straight, clear and fine as an upland wind and summer sun"; of the Scandinavian note—"one got a sense in those countries of the most advanced civilization, yet without sophistication, a luminous modern intelligence that selected and controlled and did not allow itself to be overwhelmed by the chaos of twentieth century possibility"? We see things in that white light only when they have some deeply personal meaning for us, and Bourne's instinct had led him straight to his mark. Two complex impressions he had gained that were to dominate all his later work. One was the sense of what a national culture is, of its immense value and significance as a source and fund of spiritual power even in a young world committed to a political and economic internationalism. The other was a keen realization of the almost apostolic rôle of the young student class in perpetuating, rejuvenating, vivifying and, if need be, creating this national consciousness. No young Hindu ever went back to India, no young Persian or Ukrainian or Balkan student ever went home from a European year with a more fervent sense of the chaos and spiritual stagnation and backwardness of his own people, of the happy responsibility laid upon himself and all those other young men and women who had been touched by the modern spirit.

It was an interesting moment. Never had we realized so keenly the spiritual inadequacy of American life: the great war of the cultures left us literally gasping in the vacuum of our own provincialism, colonialism, naïveté and romantic self-complacency. We were in much the same position as that of the Scandinavian countries during the European wars of 1866-1870, if we are to accept George Brandes' description of it: "While the intellectual life languished, as a plant droops in a close, confined place, the people were self-satisfied. They rested on their laurels and fell into a doze. And while they dozed they had dreams. The cultivated, and especially the half-cultivated, public in Denmark and Norway dreamed that they were the salt of Europe. They dreamed that by their idealism they would regenerate the foreign nations. They dreamed that they were the free, mighty North, which would lead the cause of the peoples to victory—and they woke up unfree, impotent, ignorant." It was through a great effort of social introspection that Scandinavia had roused itself from the stupor of this optimistic idealism, and at last a similar movement was on foot in America. *The New Republic* had started with the war, *The Masses* was still young, *The Seven Arts* and the new *Dial* were on the horizon. Bourne found himself instantly in touch with the purposes of all these papers, which spoke of a new class-consciousness, a sort of offensive and defensive alliance of the younger intelligentsia and the awakened elements of the labor groups. His audience was awaiting him, and no one could have been better prepared to take advantage of it.

It was not merely the exigencies of journalism that turned his mind at first so largely to the problems of primary education. In Professor Dewey's theories, in the Gary Schools, he saw, as he could see it nowhere else, the definite promise, the actual unfolding of the freer, more individualistic, and at the same time more communistic social life of which he dreamed. But even if he had not come to feel a certain inadequacy in Professor Dewey's point of view, I doubt if this field of interest could have held him long. Children fascinated him; how well he understood them we can see from his "Ernest: or Parent for a Day." But Bourne's heart was too insistently involved in the situation of his own contemporaries, in the stress of their immediate problems, to allow him to linger in these long hopes. This younger intelligentsia in whose ultimate unity he had had such faith—did he not see it, moreover, as the war advanced, lapsing, falling apart again, reverting into the ancestral attitudes of the tribe? Granted the war, it was the business of these liberals to see that it was played, as he said, "with insistent care for democratic values at home, and unequivocal alliance with democratic elements abroad for a peace that should promise more than a mere union of benevolent imperialisms." Instead, the "allure of the martial" passed only to be succeeded by the "allure of the technical," and the "prudent, enlightened college man," cut in the familiar pattern, took the place of the value-creator, the path-finder, the seeker of new horizons. Plainly, the younger generation had not begun to find its own soul, had hardly so much as registered its will for a new orientation of the American spirit.

Had it not occurred before, this general reversion to type? The whole first phase of the social movement had spent itself in a sort of ineffectual beating of the air, and Bourne saw that only through a far more heroic effort of criticism than had yet been attempted could the young intelligentsia disentangle itself, prevail against the mass-fatalism of the middle class, and rouse the workers out of their blindness and apathy. Fifteen years ago a new breath had blown over the American scene: people felt that the era of big business had reached its climacteric, that a new nation was about to be born out of the social settlements, out of the soil that had been harrowed and swept by the muckrakers, out of the spirit of "service" that animated a whole new race of novelists; and a vast army of young men and women, who felt fluttering in their souls the call to some great impersonal adventure, went forth to the slums and the factories and the universities with a powerful but very vague desire to realize themselves and to "do something" for the world. But one would have said that movement had been born middle-aged, so earnest, so anxious, so conscientious, so troubled, so maternal and paternal were the faces of those young men and women who marched forth with so puzzled an intrepidity; there was none of the tang and fire of youth in it, none of the fierce glitter of the intellect, no joyous burning of boats, no transfiguration. There was only a warm simmer of eager, evangelical sentiment that somehow never reached the boiling-point and cooled rapidly off again, and that host of tentative and wistful seekers found themselves as cruelly astray as the visionaries of the Children's Crusade. Was not the failure of that movement due almost wholly to its lack of critical equipment? It was too naïve and provincial, it was outside the main stream of modern activity and desire, it had none of the reserves of power that result from being in touch with contemporary developments in other countries. Those crusaders of the "social consciousness" were far from being conscious of themselves; they had never broken the umbilical cord of their class, they had not discovered their own individual lines of growth, they had no knowledge of their own powers, no technique for using them effectively. Embarked in activities that revealed themselves as futile and fallacious, they also found their loyalties in conflict with one another. Inevitably their zeal waned and their energy ebbed away, and the tides of uniformity and commercialism swept the scene once more.

No one had grasped all these elements of the social situation so firmly as Bourne. He saw that we needed, first, a psychological interpretation of these younger malcontents; secondly, a realistic study of our institutional life; and finally, a general opening of the American mind to the currents of contemporary desire and effort and experiment abroad. And along each of these lines he did the work of a pioneer.

Who, for instance, had ever thought of exploring the soul of the younger generation as Bourne explored it? He had planned a long series of literary portraits of its types and personalities: half a dozen of them exist, enough to show us how sensitively he responded to those detached, groping, wistful, yet resolutely independent spirits whom he saw weaving the fabric of the future. He who had so early divined the truth of Maurice Barrès' saying, that we never conquer the intellectual suffrages of those who precede us in life, addressed himself exclusively to these young spirits. He went out to meet them, he probed their obscurities: one would have said that he was a sort of impresario gathering an orchestra, seeking in each the principle of his own growth. He had studied his chosen minority with such instinctive care that everything he wrote came as a personal message to those, and those alone, who were capable of assimilating it; and that is why, as we look over his writings today, we find them a sort of corpus, a text full of secret ciphers, and packed with meaning between the lines, of all the most intimate questions and difficulties and turns of thought and feeling that make up the soul of young America. He revealed us to ourselves, he intensified and at the same time corroborated our desires; above all, he showed us what we had in common and what new increments of life might rise out of the friction of our differences. In these portraits he was already doing the work of the novelist he might well have become: he left, in fact, two or three chapters of a novel he had begun to write, in which "Karen" and "Sopronisba" and "The Professor" would probably have appeared, along with a whole battle-array of the older and younger generations. Everything for analysis, for self-discovery, everything to put the younger generation in possession of itself! Everything to weave the tissue of a common understanding! There was something prophetic in Bourne's personality. In his presence, in his writings one felt that the army of youth was assembling for the "effort of reason and the adventure of beauty."

I shall say little of his work as a critic of institutions. It is enough to point out that if such realistic studies as his "Trans-National America" and his "Mirror of the Middle West" (a perfect example, by the way, of his theory of the book review as an independent enquiry with a central idea of its own), his papers on the settlements and on sociological fiction had appeared fifteen years ago, a vastly greater amount of effective energy might have survived the break-up of the first phase of the social movement. When he showed what mare's-nests the settlements and the "melting-pot" theory and the "spirit of service" are, and what snares for democracy lie in Meredith Nicholson's "folksiness," he closed the gate on half the blind alleys in which youth had gone astray; and he who had so delighted in Veblen's ruthless condensation of the mystical gases of American business implied in every line he wrote that there is a gulf fixed between the young intellectual and the unreformable "system." The young intellectual, henceforth, was an unclassed outsider, with a scent all the more keenly sharpened for new trails because the old trails were denied him; and for Bourne those new trails led straight, and by the shortest possible route, to a society the very reverse of ours, a society such as A. E. has described in the phrase, "democratic in economics, aristocratic in thought," to be attained through a coalition of the thinkers and the workers. The task of the thinkers, in so far as they concerned themselves directly with economic problems, was, in Bourne's eyes, chiefly to *think*. It was a new doctrine for American radicals; it precisely denoted their advance over the evangelicism of fifteen years ago. "The young radical of today," he wrote in one of his reviews, "is not asked to be a martyr, but he is asked to be a thinker, an intellectual leader.... The labor movement in this country needs a philosophy, a literature, a constructive socialist analysis and criticism of industrial relations. Labor will scarcely do this thinking for itself. Unless middle-class radicalism threshes out its categories and interpretations and undertakes this constructive thought it will not be done.... The only way in which middle-class radicalism can serve is by being fiercely and concentratedly intellectual."

Finally, through Bourne more than through any other of our younger writers one gained a sense of the stir of the great world, of the currents and cross-currents of the contemporary European spirit, behind and beneath the war, of the tendencies and experiences and common aims and bonds of the younger generation everywhere. He was an exception to what seems to be the general rule, that Americans who are able to pass outside their own national spirit at all are apt to fall headlong into the national spirit of some one other country: they become vehement partisans of Latin Europe, or of England or Russia, or of Germany and Scandinavia. Bourne, with that singular union of detachment and affectionate penetration which he brought also to his personal relationships, had entered them all with an equal curiosity, an impartial delight. If he had absorbed the fine idealism of the English liberals, he understood also the more elemental impulse of revolutionary Russia. He was full of practical suggestions from the vast social laboratory of modern Germany. He had caught something also from the intellectual excitement of young Italy; most of all, his imagination had been captivated, as we can see from such essays as "Mon Amie," by the candor of the French and their genius for social introspection. These influences were all perpetually at play in his writings. He was the conductor of innumerable diverse inspirations, a sort of clearing-house of the best living ideas of the time; through him the young writer and the young thinker came into instant contact with whatever in the modern world he most needed. And here again Bourne revealed his central aim. He reviewed by choice, and with a special passion, what he called the "epics of youthful talent that grows great with quest and desire." It is easy to see, in his articles on such books as "Pelle the Conqueror" and Gorky's Autobiography, that what attracted him was the common struggle and aspiration of youth and poverty and the creative spirit everywhere, the sense of a new socialized world groping its way upward. It was this rich ground-note in all his work that made him, not the critic merely, but the leader.

It is impossible to say, of course, what he would have become had his life been spared. The war had immensely stimulated his "political-mindedness." He was obsessed, during the last two years of his life, with a sense of the precariousness of free thought and free speech in this country; if they were cut off, he foresaw, the whole enterprise of the new American culture would perish of inanition. He felt himself at bay. Would he, with all the additional provocation of a bungled peace settlement, have continued in the political field, as his unfinished study on "The State" might suggest? Or would that activity have subsided into a second place beside his more purely cultural interests?

Personally, I like to think that he would have followed this second course. He speaks in the "History of a Literary Radical" of "living down the new orthodoxies of propaganda" as he and his friends had lived down the old orthodoxies of the classics, and I believe that, freed from the obsessions of the war, his criticism would have concentrated more and more on the problem of evoking and shaping an American literature as the nucleus of that rich, vital and independent national life he had been seeking in so many ways to promote. Who that knew his talent could have wished it otherwise? Already, except for the poets, the intellectual energy of the younger generation has been drawn almost exclusively into political interests; and the new era, which has begun to draw so sharply the battle-line between radicals and reactionaries, is certain only to increase this tendency.[1] If our literary criticism is always impelled sooner or later to become social criticism, it is certainly because the future of our literature and art depends upon the wholesale reconstruction of a social life all the elements of which are as if united in a sort of conspiracy against the growth and freedom of the spirit. We are in the position described by Ibsen in one of his letters, "I do not think it is of much use

---

[1] No prophecy could have seemed more plausible when this essay was written (1919). But as Mr. Alfred Stieglitz once remarked, we have a new generation in this country every four years.

to plead the cause of art with arguments derived from its own nature, which with us is still so little understood, or rather so thoroughly misunderstood.... My opinion is that at the present time it is of no use to wield one's weapons *for* art; one must simply turn them *against* what is hostile to art." That is why Bourne, whose ultimate interest was always artistic, found himself a guerilla fighter along the whole battlefront of the social revolution. He was drawn into the political arena as a skilful specialist, called into war service, is drawn into the practice of a general surgery in which he may indeed accomplish much, but only at the price of the suspension of his own uniqueness. Others, at the expiration of what was for him a critical moment, might have been trusted to do his political work for him; his unique function, meanwhile, was not political but spiritual. It was the creation, the communication, of what he called "the allure of fresh and true ideas, of free speculation, of artistic vigor, of cultural styles, of intelligence suffused by feeling and feeling given fibre and outline by intelligence." Was it not to have been hoped, therefore, that he would have revived, exemplified among these new conditions, the long-forgotten rôle of the man of letters?

For if he held a hammer in one hand, he held in the other, a divining-rod. He, if anyone, in the days to come, would have conjured out of our dry soil the green shoots of a beautiful and a characteristic literature: he knew that soil so well, and why it was dry, and how it ought to be irrigated! We have had no chart of our cultural situation to compare with his "History of a Literary Radical," and certainly no one has combined with an analytical gift like his, and an adoration for the instinct of workmanship, so burning an eye for every stir of life and color on the drab American landscape. I think of a sentence in one of his reviews: "The appearance of dramatic imagination in any form in this country is something to make us all drop our work and run to see." That was the spirit which animated all his criticism. Is it not the spirit that creates out of the void the thing it contemplates?

THE LETTERS OF AMBROSE BIERCE

THE LETTERS OF AMBROSE BIERCE

THE Book Club of California has done a service to all lovers of good writing and fine printing in issuing a collection of the letters of Ambrose Bierce, and I wish it were possible for more readers to possess themselves of the book. Few better craftsmen in words than Bierce have lived in this country, and his letters might well have introduced him to the larger public that, even now, scarcely knows his name. A public of four hundred, however, if it happens to be a picked public, is a possession not to be despised, for the cause of an author's reputation is safer in the hands of a few Greeks than in those of a multitude of Persians. "It is not the least pleasing of my reflections," Bierce himself remarks, "that my friends have always liked my work—or me— well enough to want to publish my books at their own expense." His wonderful volume of tales, "In the Midst of Life," was rejected by virtually every publisher in the country: the list of the sponsors of his other books is a catalogue of unknown names, and the collected edition of his writings might almost have been regarded as a secret among friends. "Among what I may term 'underground reputations'," Mr. Arnold Bennett once observed, "that of Ambrose Bierce is perhaps the most striking example." The taste, the skill and the devotion with which his letters have been edited indicate, however, that, limited as this reputation is, it is destined for a long and healthy life.

It must be said at once that all the letters in the volume were written after the author's fiftieth year. They thus throw no light upon his early career, upon his development, or even upon the most active period of his creative life, for in 1893 he had already ceased to write stories. Moreover, virtually all these letters are addressed to his pupils, as he called them, young men and women who were interested in writing, and to whom he liked nothing better than to give advice. We never see him among his equals, his intimates or his contemporaries; he appears as the benevolent uncle of the gifted beginner, and we receive a perhaps quite erroneous impression that this, in his later life, was Bierce's habitual rôle. Had he no companions of his own age, no ties, no society? A lonelier man, if we are to accept the testimony of this book, never existed. He speaks of having met Mark Twain, and he refers to two or three Californian writers of the older generation; he lived for many years in Washington, chiefly, as one gathers, in the company of other old army men, few of whom had ever heard that he had written a line; he mentions Percival Pollard. Otherwise he appears to have had no friends in the East, while with the West, with San Francisco at least, he seems to have been on the worst conceivable terms. San Francisco, his home for a quarter of a century, he describes as "the paradise of ignorance, anarchy and general yellowness. . . . It needs," he remarks elsewhere, "another quake, another whiff of fire, and—more than all else—a steady trade-wind of grapeshot." It was this latter—grapeshot is just the word—that Bierce himself poured into that "moral penal colony," the worst, as he avers, "of all the Sodoms and Gomorrahs in our modern world"; and his collection of satirical epigrams shows us how much he detested it. To him San Francisco was all that London was to Pope, the Pope of "The Dunciad"; but it was a London without any delectable Twickenham villas or learned Dr. Arbuthnots or gay visiting Voltaires.

To the barrenness of his environment is to be

attributed, no doubt, the trivial and ephemeral character of so much of his work; for while his interests were parochial, his outlook, as these letters reveal it, was broadly human. With his air of a somewhat dandified Strindberg he combined what might be described as a temperament of the eighteenth century. It was natural to him to write in the manner of Pope: lucidity, precision, "correctness" were the qualities he adored. He was full of the pride of individuality; and the same man who spent so much of his energy "exploring the ways of hate" was, in his personal life, the serenest of stoics. The son of an Ohio farmer, he had had no formal education. How did he acquire such firmness and clarity of mind? He was a natural aristocrat, and he developed a rudimentary philosophy of aristocracy which, under happier circumstances, might have made him a great figure in the world of American thought. But the America of his day was too chaotic. It has remained for Mr. Mencken to develop and popularize, with more learning but with less refinement, the views that Bierce expressed in "The Shadow on the Dial."

Some of these views appear in his letters, enough to show us how complete was his antipathy to the dominant spirit of the age. He disliked humanitarianism as much as he liked humanism, or would have liked it if he had had the opportunity. He invented the word peasant in Mr. Mencken's sense, as applied, that is, to such worthies as James Whitcomb Riley. "The world does not wish to be helped," he says. "The poor wish only to be rich, which is impossible, not to be better. They would like to be rich in order to be worse, generally speaking." His contempt for socialism was unbounded. Of literary men holding Tolstoy's views he remarks that they are not artists at all: "They are 'missionaries' who, in their zeal to lay about them, do not scruple to seize any weapon that they can lay their hands on; they would grab a crucifix to beat a dog. The dog is well beaten, no doubt (which makes him a worse dog than he was before), but note the condition of the crucifix!" All this in defence of literature and what he regards as its proper function. Of Shaw and, curiously, Ibsen, he observes that they are "very small men, pets of the drawing-room and gods of the hour"; he abhors Whitman, on the score equally of sentiment and form; and of Mr. Upton Sinclair's early hero he writes as follows:

> I suppose there are Arthur Sterlings among the little fellows, but if genius is not serenity, fortitude and reasonableness I don't know what it is. One cannot even imagine Shakespeare or Goethe bleeding over his work and howling

when "in the fell clutch of circumstance." The great ones are figured in my mind as ever smiling—a little sadly at times, perhaps, but always with conscious inaccessibility to the pinpricking little Titans that would storm their Olympus armed with ineffectual disasters and popgun misfortunes. Fancy a fellow wanting, like Arthur Sterling, to be supported by his fellows in order that he may write what they don't want to read!

Bierce was consistent: his comments on his own failure to achieve recognition are all in the spirit of this last contemptuous remark. "I have pretty nearly ceased to be 'discovered'," he writes to one of his friends, "but my notoriety as an obscurian may be said to be worldwide and apparently everlasting." Elsewhere, however, he says: "It has never seemed to me that the 'unappreciated genius' had a good case to go into court with, and I think he should be promptly non-suited. . . . Nobody compels us to make things that the world does not want. We merely choose to because the pay, *plus* the satisfaction, exceeds the pay alone that we get from work that the world does want. Then where is our grievance? We get what we prefer when we do good work; for the lesser wage we do easier work." Sombre and at times both angry and cynical as Bierce's writing may seem, no man was ever freer from personal bitterness.

THE LETTERS OF AMBROSE BIERCE

If he was out of sympathy with the life of his time and with most of its literature, he adored literature itself, according to his lights. It is this dry and at the same time whole-souled enthusiasm that makes his letters so charming. Fortunate was the circle of young writers that possessed so genial and so severe a master.

One forms the most engaging picture of the old man "wearing out the paper and the patience" of his friends, reading to them Mr. Ezra Pound's "Ballade of the Goodly Fere." Where poetry is in question, no detail is too small to escape his attention, no day long enough for the counsel and the appreciation he has to give. "I don't worry about what my contemporaries think of me," he writes to his favorite pupil. "I made 'em think of *you*—that's glory enough for one." Every page of his book bears witness to the sincerity of this remark. Whether he is advising his "little group of gifted obscurians" to read Landor, Pope, Lucian, or Burke, or elucidating some point of style, or lecturing them on the rudiments of grammar, or warning them against the misuse of literature as an instrument of reform, or conjuring them not to "edit" their thought for somebody whom it may pain, he exemplifies his own dicta, that, on the one hand, "literature and art are about all that the world really cares for in the end," and on the other that, in considering the work of his friends, a critic should "keep his heart out of his head." Let me quote two or three other observations:

> One cannot be trusted to feel until one has learned to think.
>
> Must one be judged by his average, or may he be judged, on occasion, by his highest? He is strongest who can lift the greatest weight, not he who habitually lifts lesser ones.
>
> A writer should, for example, forget that he is an American and remember that he is a man. He should be neither Christian, nor Jew, nor Buddhist, nor Mohammedan, nor Snake Worshipper. To local standards of right and wrong he should be civilly indifferent. In the virtues, so-called, he should discern only the rough notes of a general expediency; in fixed moral principles only time-saving predecisions of cases not yet before the court of conscience. Happiness should disclose itself to his enlarging intelligence as the end and purpose of life; art and love as the only means to happiness. He should free himself of all doctrines, theories, etiquettes, politics, simplifying his life and mind, attaining clarity with breadth and unity with height.

This is evidently a "set piece"; but behind its rhetoric one discerns the feeling of a genuine humanist.

In certain ways, to be sure, this is a sad book.

THE LETTERS OF AMBROSE BIERCE

At seventy-one Bierce set out for Mexico "with a pretty definite purpose," as he wrote, "which, however, is not at present disclosable." From this journey he never returned, nor since 1913, has any word ever been received from him. What was that definite purpose? What prompted him to undertake so mysterious an expedition? Was it the hope of exchanging death by "old age, disease, or falling down the cellar stairs" for the "euthanasia" of death in action? He had come to loathe the civilization in which he lived, and his career had been a long tale of defeat. Of journalism he said that it is "a thing so low that it cannot be mentioned in the same breath with literature"; nevertheless, to journalism he had given nine-tenths of his energy. It is impossible to read his letters without feeling that he was a starved man; but certainly it can be said that, if his generation gave him very little, he succeeded in retaining in his own life the poise of an Olympian.

AMOR FATI

AMOR FATI

IN one of his recent essays, Mr. Santayana speaks of the immense value in the world of thought of a complete indifference to forms of life that are beyond one's power of realization. He is discussing snobs and snobbishness; and he suggests, apropos of the instinct of social emulation, that nothing could be better calculated to advance the material well-being of society: it is in ages and among races in which that instinct is weakest, on the other hand, that we find the most marked variations in the sphere of the intellect. Mr. Santayana cites the Hindus who roll in the dust, rapt in their separate universes, oblivious of the destiny of king or merchant; but we do not need to go to Asia to perceive that nothing is more advantageous in the life of thought than a certain fatalism in all mundane affairs. It has been plausibly argued that the decline of English letters dates from the hour when the writer was enabled to compete with the gentleman. Charles

Lamb and his circle, for example, knew nothing of that social aspiration which has had such an ill effect on their successors; and who will deny that what we call "opportunity" has had much to do with retarding the development of our own literature? Man is a being that thinks, but only by compulsion; and when there are so many open paths to fortune why should he subject himself to that discomfort which, as Renan said, is the principle of movement? For this reason, the closing of the American frontier may fairly be taken to portend a certain intensification in our literary life.

The probability is, indeed, that as long as other and more natural forms of life are not beyond one's power of realization, the mind cannot be quite indifferent to them. If that is true, the absence of caste in our civilization is a positive detriment to literature; for writers, like all craftsmen, are happiest when they possess a sphere of their own, a self-sufficient sphere out of which they are never tempted to stray. That ancient tag about "the world forgetting, by the world forgot" really states the first principle of the conservation of energy in the literary life: such modern writers as Thomas Hardy and George Gissing exemplify it, and it was their acting on this principle that justified, as the late

AMOR FATI

Alexander Teixeira de Mattos observed in one of his recently published letters, so many of the "men of the 'nineties." They "hadn't clubs, homes, wives or children," he says; they "lunched for a shilling, dined for eighteen pence, and didn't want a lot of money. They cared neither for money nor fame; they cared for their own esteem and that of what you call their coterie and I their set." There we have the guild-spirit, the pride of the *métier,* out of which the art and literature of the past have come; but how far has not that pride been a consequence of the stratification of life in societies in which the individual has had virtually no chance of "rising in the world"? That heights can exist, as it were, at every social level is a notion that seems to lodge only in minds that accept their level as predetermined. Thus the extremity of the old Adam is the opportunity of the new; and we may say that the star of hope rose over our literature on the day when the last barefoot boy in Missouri ceased to dream of inhabiting the White House.

It is certainly true that the writers of our generation have, as a class, begun to accept their fate. They have seceded, that is, from the bouregoisie, and ceased to accept the verdict of their bankers as the last word on their own success or failure. Henry Adams remarked that the American mind of his day had less respect for money than the European or Asiatic mind, and bore its loss more easily; but he added that it had been deflected by the pursuit of money "till it could turn in no other direction." We can see the result in the American literature of the generation preceding the war: it was characteristic of the age of the 'best sellers' that the chief preoccupation of its authors was the maintenance of a "standard of living," and few were those who were not driven by the fear of dropping behind in the race. That essentially alien idea, to the pursuit of which we can trace the exaggerated "inferiority-complex" of the American writer as a type—for how can artists compete with captains of industry and preserve their self-respect?—that alien idea no longer dominates our literary life. Our chief difficulty is that as yet no other ideal has taken its place.

The historians of the next generation who look back upon the literature of our day will find in it all the traits of an interregnum of ideals. It will appear as marked, that is, by the habits of mind of the preceding epoch, oddly disoriented, fading, dissolving, undergoing all manner of transmutations; it will seem to bear a sort of intermediate character, as between a pioneer literature and a high literature in the proper sense. It is, in other words, the expression of a will to create in minds imperfectly adapted to the creative life. The assumed necessity of having to justify themselves financially, to conform to public opinion, to be useful and to produce only the useful, combine to prevent American writers from accepting their status and making a fine art of it. They have at bottom the mental constitutions of practical men; and an ingrained need of the approval of the majority stands in the way of their strongest conscious desires. Hence the egomania of our contemporaries, their itch for publicity, their haunting fear of not being known, their anxiety to keep up with every new idea, every new movement.

In the normal course of things, the conscious cravings of one generation are likely to become the unconscious impulsions of the next. The passionate material desires of fifty years ago have passed below the threshold of the consciousness of our epoch. Meanwhile, the typical minds of our day, moved by those desires, have been filled with desires of a very different order. When the latter have been ploughed under the soil, we may expect a genuine literary movement in this country: all the signs seem to point that way. In things of the mind, however, nothing is automatic; and the American Renaissance will not get very far unless it develops the guild-spirit in place of the spirit of log-rolling. The bad habits of the writers of today are due to the precariousness of their situation. Our society is so chaotic that they cannot feel they are voicing anything but their individual sentiments, and for this reason they lack confidence in themselves. Towards the organization of society, which is indispensable as the condition of a high literature, they can contribute very little; but the development of a craft-sense, a sense of the art, not only of writing but of being a writer, is within their power; and by means of it they can prepare for the hour when society has need of them, and perhaps hasten its coming. By doing so they will escape from that state of unstable equilibrium in which they now achieve so little that is good. "Let each one ask himself," said Goethe, "for what he is best fitted, and let him cultivate this most ardently and wisely in himself and for himself; let him consider himself successively as apprentice, as journeyman, as older journeyman, and finally, but with the greatest circumspection, as master." How different this attitude is, and how much more productive, than the prevailing attitude of our

AMOR FATI

well-intentioned contemporaries. Strictly speaking, however, it is one of the logical consequences, in a human nature that exists by faith and will, of the necessity of accepting a limited status in life.

NOTES ON HERMAN MELVILLE

NOTES ON HERMAN MELVILLE

I

ALFRED DE MUSSET complained that he had been born too late in a world too old. Melville was born too soon in a world too young. While he lived he was known chiefly, till he ceased to be known at all, as "the man who had lived among the cannibals." That he was a genius of a high order seems to have escaped even his few warm admirers, who regarded him as at best a kind of superior Clark Russell. Melville was embittered by this neglect and misunderstanding. "Though I wrote the gospels in this century," he said, "I should die in the gutter." He had a high pride in his own powers, as we can see, for instance, from the concluding chapters of "Pierre"; and it seemed to him as plain as it seemed to Pierre that "though the world worship Mediocrity and Commonplace, yet hath it fire and sword for all contemporary Grandeur." But at bottom he seems to have had some confidence in the ultimate restoration of his fame. To Hawthorne he wrote that he expected to go down to some of the babies who would be born an hour after his death. More significant still are the comments of the sages in "Mardi" on the great Lombardo's "Kostanza," that mighty epic condemned in its own generation. "It was written with a divine intent," says one. "It has bettered my heart," says another. "And I have read it through nine times," says a third. "Ah, Lombardo," says Babbalanja, starting up. "This must make thy ghost glad!"

Melville has come back at last. He has come back, moreover, as the author not merely of "Typee," "Omoo" and "Moby-Dick," but of "White Jacket" and "Redburn," which might well have been popular classics all these years, as well as the apocryphal books, as I can only call them. By these I mean "Mardi," "Pierre" and "The Confidence Man: His Masquerade." The first of these works, "Typee," was published in 1846. "The Confidence Man" appeared in 1857, when its author was thirty-eight. Eleven years was thus virtually the whole span of Melville's literary life; and never, surely, in so short a time has a mind undergone a more singular transformation. As we survey these books in conjunction it becomes clearer than ever that "Moby-Dick" is Melville's one masterpiece; but none of them is entirely negligible, and all, to say the least, throw some light on the history and the quality of their author's mind. We can understand as we read them successively why it was that Melville seemed to his contemporaries such an enigma. The whole tendency of his work was, in the first place, an implicit assault on the doctrine of progress as the nineteenth century conceived it. He never hesitated to say that he had found the civilized white man "the most ferocious animal on the face of the earth." He pictured the savages of the South Seas not as the rudimentary Europeans that people liked to think them, but as the masters of an art of living in many ways incomparably superior to ours. Such things were hard to forgive; and harder still, in a hopeful age, was the note of tragic scepticism that reverberated through his work. I say nothing of the increasing incomprehensibility of his speculations: he seemed to have abandoned himself to some wilful passion for "remote and curious allusions, wrecks of forgotten fables, antediluvian computations, obsolete and unfamiliar problems, riddles that no living Œdipus would care to solve"; and all this within scarcely more than a decade.

He was, like his own "Pierre," a tropical author. He had, that is, a precocious, one might almost say a furious development; and he passed, while still young, to the confusion of himself as well as of his readers, into a long night of the soul.

I touch here upon some of the interesting questions that no reader of Melville can disregard. But first, to turn to his books: if "Moby-Dick" is his one supreme achievement, it is because here, and here alone, the subjective and objective elements in his mind approach some sort of equilibrium. "Redburn" and "White Jacket," like "Typee" and "Omoo," are simple chronicles. Nothing could be better of its kind than the first of these books, the "sailor-boy confessions and reminiscences of the son of a gentleman in the merchant service." It is really the account of Melville's first voyage when, at seventeen, he set out from his home near Albany and enlisted as a seaman on a ship from Liverpool. Nowhere else has he written with higher spirits: his picture of a sailor's New York, of Liverpool in 1837, of his adventures on the "Highlander" are all in the liveliest style of picaresque narrative. One is not likely to forget the macabre episode of the dead sailor in the bunk, whose body, at the approach of the lamp, burned "like a phosphorescent shark in a midnight sea," or the masterly portrait of Jackson, the bully with the snaky eye and the face as yellow as gamboge who bedevils the whole crew and meets with such an appalling retribution. Here too we find that delight in health and physical beauty which is one of the bonds between Melville and Walt Whitman. "Moby-Dick" is full of this delight. One remembers the picture of the gigantic Negro Daggoo with little Flask mounted like a snowflake on his back: "Sustaining himself with a cool, indifferent, easy, unthought-of, barbaric majesty, the noble Negro to every roll of the sea harmoniously rolled his fine form." And the passage in which Melville exults in his own robustness: "A thin joist of a spine never yet upheld a full and noble soul. I rejoice in my spine, as in the firm audacious staff of that flag which I fling half out to the world." And that other passage where he celebrates the massive chest of Goethe and the tendons of Hercules and the muscularity of Michaelangelo's God. One recalls too, in "Redburn," the description of the little Sicilian organ-grinder—Whitman would have written it differently, but he would have felt it in much the same way:

From the knee downward, the naked leg was beautiful

to behold as any lady's arms; so soft and rounded, with infantile ease and grace. His whole figure was free, fine and indolent; he was such a boy as might have ripened into life in a Neapolitan vineyard; such a boy as gypsies steal in infancy; such a boy as Murillo often painted, when he went among the poor and outcast for subjects wherewith to captivate the eyes of rank and wealth; such a boy as only Andalusian beggars are, full of poetry, gushing from every rent.

Of "White Jacket" not so much can be said. It tells us more about Melville himself, but it is not so good a book. Its purpose was to "give some idea of the interior life in a man-of-war," and it is based on Melville's observations in the year 1843 which he spent as a seaman on the frigate "United States." Here we meet "noble Jack Chase," the perfect sailor, with the clear eye, the fine, broad brow and the abounding nut-brown beard, the frank and charming Jack, oracle of the maintop, idol of the men, who could speak five languages and recite the "Lusiad" in the original and who was, in fact, "better than a hundred common mortals." The portrait of Jack Chase stands beside that of Jackson; but the book itself, competent as it is, is as much inferior to "Redburn" as "Omoo" is to "Typee." It is a loose exposition rather than a well-knit narrative; but it deserves to live, side by side with "Two Years Before the Mast," as the record of an aspect of life that will never have such another chronicler. What remains, aside from the Polynesian voyages, among the books that may be called objective? "The Piazza Tales," perhaps; certainly "Israel Potter." In the first we find "Benito Cereno," the story of a mutiny on a South American ship, and "Bartleby," a fantastic character-study, somewhat in the manner of Dickens. The second is a freely rendered biography of a Green Mountain boy who was captured by the British in the Revolution and carried to England: there he escaped, acted as an emissary for Franklin in Paris, fought with Paul Jones, lived for half a century in poverty in London, and came home to America, a Rip van Winkle, just in time to die.

So much for the simple tales, transcripts, for the most part, of the author's experience. "The Confidence Man" is an abortion: it is broken off in the middle, apparently, but not before the author has lost the thread of his original idea. Is it possible that, in a second volume, he might have recovered himself? We can only say that the satire is lost in a fog of undirected verbiage; but how bright is the scene when, at moments, the fog lifts, and how admirable is the vision that we seem to see laboring to be born in its baffled author's brain! A mysterious stranger, apparently deaf and dumb, boards a Mississippi steamboat just after a placard has been posted offering a reward for the apprehension of a notorious confidence-man who is believed to be in the neighborhood. The stranger stands for a moment beside the placard, writes on a slate so that all may see it the legend "Charity thinketh no evil"; then he retires to a remote corner of the deck and falls asleep. Presently, one after another, as the boat sails down the river, a Negro cripple, a man in mourning, a man in gray, a brisk man with a travelling-cap, a stranger in a snuff-colored surtout, an herb-doctor appear in various parts of the deck and cabins, convince their listeners that they ought to have "confidence" in life, and incidentally in the Omni-Balsamic Re-invigorator, in the stock of the Black Rapids Coal Company, in the Widow and Orphan Asylum for the Seminoles, in the virtues of the Philosophical Intelligence Office: and invariably succeed in collecting a number of dollars. This is the "masquerade" of the confidence-man; and we can see that Melville intended to satirize the follies and illusions of humanity while conveying, at the same time, the gist of his own philosophy. But he had lost command of his medium; and the book remains, interesting indeed, but the product of a premature artistic senility.

II

Aside from "Moby-Dick," "Mardi" and "Pierre" are Melville's most ambitious books. They seem to me, however—except for the latter chapters of "Pierre"—rather the products of his reading than of any intense personal experience. Melville says in his preface to "Mardi" that after his two early voyages in the Pacific had been received with incredulity it occurred to him to write a romance of Polynesian adventure to see whether the fiction might not be taken for truth. As a simple romance, perhaps, the book was begun; but having opened as the story of the pursuit of the girl Yillah, it presently turns into the most complicated and chaotic allegory that ever drifted through a human mind. The lost maiden may symbolize either truth or happiness—but indeed the question matters very little. Poe justly objected to the best allegory, and of "Mardi" it may be said that neither the ostensible nor the concealed meaning is presented with sufficient force to hold our attention long. In form the work is a more or less direct imitation of the fourth and fifth books of Rabelais: the narrator and his three companions, Mohy the chronicler, Babbalanja the antiquary, and Yoomy the minstrel, set out in their three canoes for a tour of the isles, and we are at once reminded of the voyage of Pantagruel, Panurge and Friar John. They are in search of Yillah as the voyagers of Rabelais are in search of the oracle of the *Dive Bouteille,* and they too pass their time in pleasant conversation. Most of this conversation may be described as "ontological heroics." It gives us a fair idea of the sort of talk that must have passed between Melville and Hawthorne.

The skeleton of the book is thus taken from Rabelais. Its imagery, on the other hand, is that of the South Seas. Melville had not forgotten the feast of calabashes in the valley of Typee and the cheerful confabulatoins of the old men gathered in the Ti. The thatched huts, the verdurous arbors, the luxuriant glens of the Marquesas are perceptible in the background; but over this etherealized scene there lingers a faint Oriental aroma as of some Mussulman paradise of Thomas Moore, and we remember that Melville had stowed away among his folios a cherished copy of "The Loves of the Angels." No doubt Moore was responsible also for the conception of Yillah, the form that Melville's fancy gave to some dim recollection perhaps of Fayaway. Yillah is of the same family as Poe's heroines, the Lenores, the Eulalies, the Ligeias, and serves to show us that this ancient mariner, who often suggests some revenant of the days of Drake and Hakluyt moving about in worlds not realized, was also a literary New Yorker of the eighteen fifties.

Melville was a natural, an unconscious artist; and such men fall an easy prey to the most casual influences. As the strongest peasants disintegrate in urban surroundings, so these apparently robust minds that have not succeeded in fortifying themselves with knowledge, the knowledge of their craft, the exact knowledge of realities, are defenceless against everything that passes on the wind. In "Moby-Dick" Melville achieved a style that is at once highly personal and a palingenesis of the grave and splendid prose of the seventeenth century. All the old plays and voyages and meditations over which he had pored as a boy and a young man, Jonson and Browne, Raleigh and Fletcher, and the Shakespeare that he had worn to a pulpy mass in his pocket, had mounted in his mind, their rhythms mingling with the remembered rhythm of the ocean, as that mighty theme possessed him. Here and there, in his other books, the mood returns at rare moments, and we have such lines as this from "White Jacket": "Let me lie down with Drake, where he sleeps in the sea." Elsewhere, the personal accent, the note of intention, of authority, vanishes; he is at the mercy of the last book he has read. The devastating effect that Carlyle had upon Melville's mind is well known. A minor instance of the same phenomenon is to be found in the form which he chose for his interminable metaphysical poem "Clarel." In "Omoo" he speaks of listening to the ship's doctor, Long Ghost, who knew "Hudibras" by heart and recited it hour after hour. It was undoubtedly thanks to this memory that, years later, he chose the metre of "Hudibras" for his own poem—an unhappy choice, for the jingling rhymes and the velocity of the style redouble the unpalatability of the subject. In "Pierre" we find still another set of influences at work. Were it possible we should suppose that Melville had read "Seraphita," for the conception of Isabel, who "seemed molded from fire and air, and vivified at some voltaic pile of August thunder-clouds heaped against the sunset," strikingly resembles that of Balzac's figure of mystery. We can only conclude that he had read the writers whom Balzac himself had read, Maturin, Mrs. Radcliffe and Monk Lewis. However this may be, we know that "Vathek" and "The Castle of Otranto" were among the books he brought back from England in 1850. To these may be traced perhaps the magniloquent, high-flown style in which he cast the story of Pierre and Isabel.

The latter chapters of "Pierre" are transparently autobiographical: they give us what we may fairly regard as a picture of the circumstances under which "Moby-Dick" was written. A complete change takes place in the style when it appears that Pierre is a writer, that he has undertaken to write an immense book, a "comprehensive compacted work," an Inferno, as it soon turns out to be; the vaporous atmosphere of the story suddenly clears, we are confronted with a scene of the most convincing reality, we feel that the author has abandoned the uncongenial task of invention, that he is speaking to us directly, describing a personal experience. As a matter of fact, the circumstances that surround the composition of Pierre's book are precisely those that accompanied the composition of Melville's. He too was obliged to send the manuscript to the printer while he was still at work on it, he too struggled against failing eyesight, he too was a victim of "clamorous pennilessness"; and we have only to recall his remark to Hawthorne that "Moby-Dick" was "broiled in hell-fire" to lose any fear of pressing the analogy too close. "All creation," said Amiel, "begins with a period of chaotic anguish. The chaos that is to give birth to a world is vast and dolorous just in proportion as the world is to be one of grandeur." Never was this better exemplified than in the case of Melville's masterpiece.

I can only recount a few details of this remarkable passage. Melville describes Pierre, in the first place, as "goaded, in the hour of mental immaturity, to the attempt at a mature work." He feels that he possesses immense inner resources; he speaks of the "Switzerland of his soul," of the "overawing extent of peak crowded on peak, and spur sloping on spur, and chain jammed behind chain." It appals him when he looks within; for equally great is the difficulty he experiences in formulating his thoughts. He feels that there are two books being written of which only the bungled one will ever reach the world. The larger book "whose unfathomable cravings drink his blood" cannot be drawn forth; it has a soul "elephantinely sluggish, and will not budge at a breath." Doubts assail him, a feeling of hopelessness and despair. His physical instincts revolt; he feels that he has assassinated the natural day; he begins to loathe his food; he cannot sleep—"his book, like a vast lumbering planet, revolves in his aching head." Then the time comes for the first pages to go to the printer:

> Thus was added still another tribulation; because the printed pages now dictated to the following manuscript, and said to all subsequent thoughts and inventions of Pierre —Thus and thus; so and so; else an ill match. Therefore was his book already limited, bound over and committed to imperfection, even before it had come to any confirmed form or conclusion at all. . . . Now he began to feel that in him the thews of a Titan were forestallingly cut by the scissors of Fate. He felt as a moose, hamstrung. All things that think, or move, or lie still, seemed as created to mock and torment him. He seemed gifted with loftiness, merely that it might be dragged down to the mud. Still, the profound wilfulness in him would not give up. Against the breaking heart and the bursting head; against all the dismal lassitude, and deathful faintness and sleeplessness, and whirlingness and craziness, still he like a demigod bore up. His soul's ship foresaw the inevitable rocks, but resolved to sail on, and make a courageous wreck. Now he gave jeer for jeer, and taunted the apes that jibed him. With the soul of an atheist, he wrote down the godliest things; with the feeling of death and misery in him, he created forms of gladness and life. . . . And everything else he disguised under the so conveniently adjustable drapery of all-stretchable Philosophy.

In the midst of this comes a final disaster—the failure of his eyesight:

> But man does never give himself up thus, a doorless and shutterless house for the four loosened winds of heaven to howl through, without still additional dilapidations. Much oftener than before, Pierre lay back in his chair with the deadly feeling of faintness. Much oftener than before, came staggering home from his evening walk, and from sheer bodily exhaustion economized the breath that answered the anxious inquiries as to what might be done for him. And as if all the leagued spiritual inveteracies and malices, combined with his general bodily exhaustion, were not enough, a special corporeal affliction now descended like a sky-hawk upon him. His incessant application told upon his eyes. They became so affected, that some days he wrote with his lids nearly closed, fearful of opening them wide to the light. Through the lashes he peered upon the paper, which so seemed fretted with wires. Sometimes he blindly wrote with his eyes turned away from the paper; thus unconsciously symbolizing the hostile necessity and distaste, the former whereof made of him this most unwilling state's-prisoner of letters. . . . And now a general and nameless torpor—some horrible foretaste of death itself—seemed stealing upon him.

Truly Melville "supped at black broth with Pluto" when he wrote "Moby-Dick."

III

Melville remains a singularly obscure figure. Of his character, his inner life, his point of view, of the catastrophic development of his mind little has been said that seems to me illuminating; yet much might be said on all these matters, might and will be said, for Melville, who was never an "eminent author," was a very great writer. We cannot penetrate the mystery of a personality. We cannot trace to its source, for example, the desperate bitterness that engulfed Melville's mind. His contempt for life, for humanity; the swift decay of his creative faculty, his madness, so to call it: these facts, beyond a certain point, transcend our powers of analysis. We can only say of Melville what he himself said of Captain Ahab, that there was a "half-wilful, overruling morbidness at the bottom of his nature."

Mr. R. M. Weaver has laid great stress on Melville's relations with his mother. It appears that as an old man he confessed that his mother had "hated" him; and we are told, we are led to suppose, that he drew her portrait in the mother of Pierre, the "haughty" Mrs. Glendinning who, when her will is crossed, disinherits her son and drives him from her house. All that we know of Melville's mother (all that seems germane, I mean) is that, in the days of his poverty, she came to live with him, and that she was "contemptuous of his domestic economy and of the home-made clothes of his four children." This certainly helps to explain his running away as a boy to sea; it seems to explain also that curious identification of himself with Ishmael—"an infant Ishmael driven out into the desert, with no maternal Hagar to accompany and comfort him"—which we find not only in "Moby-Dick" but in "Redburn" and "Pierre" as well. It was partly a love of romantic adventure that carried him to sea; but how can we ignore the plain statement in "Moby-Dick" that going to sea was his "substitute for pistol and ball," or the reference, on the first page of "Redburn," to the "sad disappointments" of his childhood? He had received some mortal hurt at the very threshold of life, and it is not for effect that we are told that Redburn had a "devil in his heart." We know these men for whom the conventional world with its "dreary heart-vacancies" is always a "wolfish world," who are soothed and mollified at the touch of the gentle savage. We know their "towering pride"—I am quoting almost at random phrases of Melville that help us to form a picture of his own character. They have been humiliated, they have been exposed too soon to the rigors of life; and, like those children for whose organisms nothing later can compensate for the original insufficiency of their mother's milk, they are all too likely to wither before their time. With what sympathy does Melville speak of Dante as having "received unforgivable affronts and insults from the world." He himself felt that every man's hand was against him; and certainly these circumstances of his childhood throw some light on the untimely eclipse of his genius.

Nor can we disregard the circumstances of his life at sea. In spite of the high spirits and the air of frankness that seem to characterize his early books, we soon discover that Melville was anything but a "jolly tar." He was a vigorous animal, but that is another matter; he liked the harsh, bracing exercises of the ship, the sting of the brine, the beating wind and that sense of the blood tingling along one's frame. But have we failed to observe with what alacrity his heroes escape from their ships, how the heroes of "Typee" and "Mardi" desert and how Melville dwells on the abuses and the miseries of the seaman's lot? "White Jacket" is almost a catalogue of these abuses: chapter after chapter is devoted to the evils of flogging, to the brutalities of surgeons and officers, to the ferocious Articles of War. And the men: Melville was the first to rejoice in a fine human specimen, a Toby or a Jack Chase, but he appears to be telling the truth when he remarks in "Typee" that the "pent-up wickedness" of the crew of a man-of-war destroyed the faith in human nature that a few weeks in the valley of the Marquesas had given him. "There are evils in men-of-war," he says, "which, like the suppressed domestic drama of Horace Walpole, will hardly bear representing, or reading, and will hardly bear thinking of." And what does he say of the crew of the "Acushnet"?—"With a very few exceptions our crew was composed of a parcel of dastardly and mean-spirited wretches, divided among themselves, and only united in enduring without resistance the unmitigated tyranny of the captain." When we consider that the whole of his later adolescence was passed amid these conditions, that from them, and virtually from them alone, his knowledge of life and the world was derived, we can understand that profound sense of the evil of the universe which marks all his later writings.

Melville was not the man to put up with the rough-and-tumble life of the ordinary sailor. As a matter of fact, he tells us repeatedly that he had few acquaintances on ship-board, that the seamen fancied that he gave himself airs. "I found myself," he says in "Redburn," "a sort of Ishmael in the ship, without a single friend or companion, and I began to feel a hatred growing up in me against the whole crew." These moods must have been frequent with him; and I think it is not unreasonable to suggest that in Captain Ahab's vindictive hatred of the white whale that symbolized life Melville vented—dramatized, so to say—the accumulated fund of bitterness, the sorrowful anger of hurt pride, the spleen, the defiant contempt that had rankled in the depths of his heart. I put this forward merely as a conjecture, for how can we demonstrate the reality of these obscure relationships of cause and effect? Meanwhile, in the peculiar solitude of this sea-life we find an explanation of Melville's subsequent development. "I am of a meditative humor," he remarks in "White Jacket," "and at sea used often to mount aloft at night, and, seating myself on one of the upper yards, tuck my jacket about me and give loose to reflection." In the light of its implications, this one sentence, I venture to say, gives us the key to the riddle of the later Melville.

"Cut off," he says, "from all those outward passing things which ashore employ the eyes, tongues and thoughts of landsmen, the inmates of a frigate are thrown upon themselves and each other, and all their ponderings are introspective." And again: "A forced, interior quietude, in the midst of great outward commotion, breeds moody people." Mr. Lincoln Colcord has shown conclusively that Melville had none of that "feeling of the sea" which is the "secret animating spring of the real sailor," that he had no professional interest in the seaman's life. Indeed, he says himself that he was "as unambitious as a man of sixty"; and who can forget that amusing passage in "Moby-Dick" in which he counsels the shipowners of Nantucket not to enlist in their vigilant fisheries romantic, melancholy and absent-minded young philosophers who would rather not see whales than otherwise and will tow you ten wakes round the world and never make you one pint of sperm the richer? What this means is that, far from drawing him out, everything, his companions, his surroundings, conspired to direct his eyes inward. "There you stand," he says in "Moby-Dick," "lost in the infinite series of the sea, with nothing ruffled but the waves. The tranced ship indolently rolls; the drowsy trade winds blow; everything resolves you into languor." Many are the pages he devotes to this "opium-like listlessness of vague unconscious reverie," pages which, in their solemn, rhythmical eloquence, are matched in modern literature only by De Quincey. Who can regret an experience that gave birth to such prose as this? We can only say that nothing is more perilous for a writer than the abyss of an emotional mysticism. In these conditions, as Melville says, one loses one's identity, one's spirit "ebbs away to whence it came, becomes diffused through time and space." One ceases in the end even to desire the narrow house of art.

"Until I was twenty-five," Melville wrote to Hawthorne in 1851, "I had no development at all. From my twenty-fifth year I date my life. Three weeks have scarcely passed, at any time between then and now, that I have not unfolded within myself. But I feel that I am now come to the inmost leaf of the bulb, and that shortly the flower must fall to the mould." Again and again he expresses these presentiments of a premature winter of the soul. In 1856 he told Hawthorne that he had "pretty much made up his mind to be annihilated." He made two journeys through the world, silently, as if looking for something; then, a Samson at the mill, a Samson without a redemption, he labored for the rest of his life in the prison-house of the Philistines. He professed not to own a copy of any of his books; when asked about his early life he replied, "That reminds me of the eighth book of Plato's Republic"; and after his death it was found that he had vigorously underscored in his copy of Schopenhauer the phrase "this hellish society of men." We are sufficiently familiar with these signs of a thwarted psyche: "It is," said Carlyle, "the one unhappiness of a man, that he cannot work, that he cannot get his destiny as a man fulfilled." In the solitude of Melville's sea-life he turned to metaphysics, he immersed himself in Hegelianism; but he had had virtually no formal education, he had undergone no intellectual discipline, and the result was inevitable. "Clear truth," as he says in "Moby-Dick," "is a thing for salamander giants only to encounter; how small the chances for the provincials then"! He fell, in short, "into Plato's honey head, and sweetly perished there."

For, as Renan has well shown, nothing can keep speculation vital but the direct study of realities. Melville was not a thinker; worse still, the only reality he knew, far from stimulating his curiosity, repelled him. It is probably true, in the first place, that a youth of excessive adventure is the worst preparation for a patient intellectual life, which inevitably seems to the mind insipid by contrast. Aside from this, aside from his failing eyesight, we gather that his personal life was a drab disappointment: he who reveals himself in "The Paradise of Bachelors" as by nature a lover of "good living, good drinking, good feeling and good talk" was all too evidently condemned to the grim, colorless, monotonous round of a small provincial existence. "One in a city of hundreds of thousands of human beings, Pierre," he says, "was solitary as at the pole. In his deepest, highest part he was utterly without sympathy from anything divine, human, brute or vegetable." He himself had had but one literary friend; and Hawthorne was no man to communicate a lively sense of terrestrial realities. Renan was right: talent is a frivolous vice. We cease to believe in it when no one shares our belief. Melville at thirty-five had outlived the literary illusion; he had come to despise the written word. We see in all this the contempt of the physical man for the work of the brain; but more still, the suffocation of a mighty genius in a social vacuum. Melville touched the uttermost note of pathetic irony when, for want of a sole articulate companion, he dedicated "Pierre" to Mount Greylock and "Israel Potter" to the Bunker Hill Monument.

IV

I wonder if, even yet, all the felicities of "Moby-Dick" have dawned on people's minds.

It seems to me now less chaotic than it seemed at first. I had taken too seriously the statement with which Melville opens one of his chapters: "There are some enterprises in which a careful disorderliness is the true method"—or rather, I had not placed enough weight on this word "careful." It seemed to me intolerable that he had not removed the chapters on whales in general, on whaling, pitchpoling, ambergris, the try-works, etc., and published them separately: they were glorious, but I could not believe that they had been deliberately introduced to retard the action. It struck me that the action should have been retarded as it were within the story. I do not feel this now. The book is an epic, and an epic requires ballast. Think of the catalogue of ships in Homer, the mass of purely historical information in the Æneid, the long descriptions in "Paradise Lost": how immensely these elements add to the density and the volume of the total impression, and how they serve to throw into relief the gestures and activities of the characters! This freight of inanimate or partially inanimate material gives "Moby-Dick" its bottom, its body, in the vintner's phrase; and I am sure that Melville knew exactly what he was about.

It is only when we have grasped the nature

of the book that we begin to see how cunning is its craftsmanship throughout. Of the larger lines I shall speak presently; but glance for a moment at the single episode of Father Mapple's sermon in the Whaleman's Chapel. Why is it that, once read, this episode seems to have built itself permanently into the tissues of our imagination? It is because of the skill with which Melville has excluded from our minds every irrelevant detail. He wishes first to establish the nautical character of the preacher, so he has him stoop down, after he has climbed into the pulpit, and drag up the ladder step by step, till the whole is deposited within. This may have been taken from reality, for Father Mapple is known to have been drawn from Father Taylor, Emerson's friend, the apostle to the sailors in Boston. But Melville's skill here consists in not remarking that Father Mapple might have been boarding a ship: the image already conveys this connotation—Melville uses it to heighten our sense of the preacher's momentary "withdrawal from all outward worldly ties and connections." And this nautical character is preserved by every detail of the sketch. When Father Mapple kneels and prays, his prayer is so deeply devout that he seems to be "kneeling and praying at the bottom of the sea." When he rises, he begins to speak "in prolonged solemn tones, like the continual tolling of a bell in a ship that is foundering at sea in a fog." This impression, once established, is maintained by the imagery of the sermon; but, to pass to another point, why do we remember the sermon so vividly? Partly because of the storm that is beating outside the chapel. We are never allowed to forget this storm. It shrieks and drives about us as we enter the chapel, it pelts the door from without, it howls between the hymn and the sermon, it appears to "add new power to the preacher, who, when describing Jonah's sea-storm, seemed tossed by a storm himself." The effect of all this is to redouble the solemn intimacy of the scene. The chapel is cut off from the world like the cabin of a ship; our minds are focussed with an almost painful intensity upon the visible and audible facts that immediately surround us.

I dwell on this episode because it shows with what deliberate art Melville has ensnared his readers. To turn now to the work as a whole, how carefully, with what prevision, he had built up the general scheme: the pitch of the book, the mystery of the White Whale, the character of Captain Ahab. First of all, the pitch—with what a mighty rhythm the "Pequod" starts on its voyage:

> Ship and boat diverged; the cold, damp night breeze blew between; a screaming gull flew overhead; the two hulls wildly rolled; we gave three heavy-hearted cheers, and blindly plunged like fate into the lone Atlantic.

There we have the note of the saga; and this is consistently sustained by a dozen different means. Take the portraits of the three mates, Starbuck, Stubb, and Flask, "momentous men" all, and the three fantastic harpooneers, the cannibal Queequog, Tashtego, the Gay Head Indian, and the gigantic Negro, Daggoo. By a process of simplification that heightens their effect without removing it from reality, Melville invests these characters with a semblance as of Homer's minor heroes:

> Daggoo retained all his barbaric virtues, and, erect as a giraffe, moved about the decks in all the pomp of six feet five in his socks. There was a corporeal humility in looking up at him; and a white man standing before him seemed a white flag come to beg truce of a fortress.

> [Tashtego.] To look at the tawny brawn of his lithe snaky limbs, you would almost have credited the superstitions of some of the earlier Puritans, and half believed this wild Indian to be a son of the Prince of the Powers of the Air.

EMERSON AND OTHERS

This method of characterization prevails throughout the book. Take the captain of the "Jeroboam," for instance:

> A long-skirted, cabalistically cut coat of a faded walnut tinge enveloped him; the overlapping sleeves of which were rolled up on his wrists. A deep, settled, fanatic delirium was in his eyes.

We are living from first to last in a world by one degree larger than life. The constant mythological allusions, the sweep of the style, the bold splendor of the similes support this impression, till at last the battles with the whales begin and we feel beneath the book the pulse of the ocean itself. "Give me a condor's wing"! Melville exclaims in the excitement of his inspiration. "Give me Vesuvius' crater for an inkstand"! And then he adds, proudly conscious of his achievement: "Such, and so magnifying, is the virtue of a large and liberal theme! We expand to its bulk. To produce a mighty book, you must choose a mighty theme."

No less extraordinary is the development of the legend of "Moby-Dick," of the sense of impending fatality. Towards the end it may be thought that Melville strains a point or two in order to produce this latter effect. I am thinking especially of the chapter in which the sea-hawk darts away with Ahab's hat; but the chapters on the "candles" and the needle are open to the same objection. There is an electrical storm and the corposants appear on the yardarms; and presently it is found that the compasses have been turned. All these phenomena are natural, but they are certainly exceptional: and, occurring so close together, they seem to me to overshoot their mark, which is, of course, to inform the reader that the calamitous whale is approaching. Machinery of this kind is much more in place in works like "The Ancient Mariner" that frankly embody supernatural elements. But consider, at the outset of the book, the apparition of Elijah. Consider that astonishing chapter on the whiteness of the whale. Consider the reports of Moby-Dick that come to us, one after another, from the sailors, from wandering sea-captains encountered during the voyage, from the mad Gabriel of the "Jeroboam," from the captain of the "Samuel Enderby" whose arm the monster has torn away as he tore away Ahab's leg. The fabulous whale torments our imagination till we, like Gabriel, think of him as "no less a being than the Shaker God incarnated"; and all this, be it noted, without a word of direct description on Melville's part. Until he reveals himself just before the chase, we see Moby-Dick solely through the consequences of his actions and the eyes of superstitious men.

One would like to linger over another aspect of the fabulous element of the book—fabulous but entirely consonant with reality. I mean the theme of the "five dusky phantoms" who appear midway in the story, suddenly surrounding Ahab and as if "fresh formed out of air." We got our first hint of their existence in the dark words of Elijah, when Ishmael and Queequeg encounter him near the wharf in the gray dawn:

> But he stole up to us again, and suddenly clapping his hand on my shoulder, said, "Did ye see anything looking like men going toward that ship a while ago?"
>
> Struck by this plain matter-of-fact question, I answered, saying, "Yes, I thought I did see four or five men; but it was too dim to be sure."
>
> "Very dim, very dim," said Elijah. "Morning to ye."
>
> Once more we quitted him; but once more he came softly after us; and touching my shoulder again, said, "See if you can find 'em now, will ye?"
>
> "Find who?"
>
> "Morning to ye! Morning to ye!" he rejoined, again moving off.

Later, on the voyage, Stubb remarks that Captain Ahab is always disappearing at night:

"Who's made appointments with him in the hold? Ain't that queer now?" These vaguely defined Orientals are satisfactorily accounted for as the story moves on; but they remain dim, and their presence and their dimness and the pale, opalescent light that emanates from them spread I can hardly say what magic through the book. Moreover, all this fantasy of "Moby-Dick" has behind it everywhere a substantial fabric of fact: that is why, at the most extravagant moments, we accept every detail as veracious. There were actually to be seen, in the Nantucket of the 'forties, such figures as Queequeg and Fedallah, just as there were old "fighting Quakers, Quakers with a vengeance," lords of whales like Bildad and Peleg, with their "thousand bold dashes of character, not unworthy a Scandinavian sea-king, or a poetical pagan Roman." We can trace the whole story, trunk, branches and twigs, back to the scene out of which it springs, just as we can trace the Arabian genie back to Aladdin's lamp.

How admirable again, in the character of Captain Ahab, is Melville's power of construction! "Ahab's soul's a centipede that moves upon a hundred legs." So he himself asseverates, in the midst of the chase; and this character of a "mighty pageant creature, formed for noble tragedies" is sustained with uncanny adroitness. First we are presented with the other captains who give us the scale of the Nantucket whalemasters in general. Then we see him through a cloud of strange rumors, and not till the ship is well at sea does he appear at all. Suddenly he emerges; he stands on the quarter-deck, and Melville describes him minutely in a magnificent passage. Then he vanishes again, to remain omnipresent but only intermittently visible, the soul, the brain, the will of the ship, and in the end the embodiment of a bedevilled humanity. We are never permitted to become familiar with him: he is never mentioned, he never appears indeed save to the accompaniment of some superb phrase, some new majestic image. He is a "grand, ungodly, god-like man," a "good man —not a pious good man, like Bildad, but a swearing good man"; he is a "khan of the plank, a king of the sea, and a great lord of leviathans"; he "lives in the world as the last of the grizzly bears lived in settled Missouri." It can fairly be said that by the time the chase begins, Ahab is as mighty and terrible a figure in our minds as Moby-Dick himself. The two fabulous characters have grown, by similar means, side by side.

Much more might be said of the form of the

book—of the shredded Shakespearean drama, for example, the scraps and fragments of which, among other diverse elements, have been pressed into the moving mass of the narrative. "The great task of an artist," said Taine, "is to find subjects which suit his talent." Melville had this fortune once and once only; but his masterpiece is worth more than libraries of lesser books. "Moby-Dick" is our sole American epic, no less an epic for being written in prose; and has it been observed that it revives in a sense the theme of the most ancient epic of the English-speaking peoples? Grendel in "Beowulf" might almost be described as the prototype of the White Whale. Was not Grendel also the symbol of "all that most maddens and torments, all that stirs up the lees of things, all truth with malice in it, all that cracks the sinews and cakes the brain, all the subtle demonisms of life and thought, all evil—visibly personified"?

THE NOVELS OF UPTON SINCLAIR

THE NOVELS OF UPTON SINCLAIR

IN 1889, when the English nation revealed through its press how unwilling it was to be "pried up to a higher level of manhood" by the "Connecticut Yankee," and was indeed denouncing the book as a travesty, Mark Twain tried to induce Andrew Lang to come to his defence. "The critic assumes, every time," he wrote, "that if a book doesn't meet the cultivated-class standard, it isn't valuable. The critic has actually impressed upon the world the superstition that a painting by Raphael is more valuable to the civilizations of the earth than is a chromo; and the august opera than the hurdy-gurdy and the villagers' singing society: and Homer than the little everybody's-poet whose rhymes are in all mouths today and will be in nobody's mouth next generation; and the Latin classics than Kipling's far-reaching bugle-note. . . . If a critic should start a religion it would not have any object but to convert angels; and they wouldn't need it.

It is not that little minority who are already saved that are best worth trying to uplift, I should think, but the mighty mass of the uncultivated who are underneath." Whereupon our troubled humorist besought Andrew Lang to "adopt a rule recognizing the Belly and the Members, and formulate a standard whereby work done for them shall be judged."

It is recorded that Andrew Lang failed to respond to this remarkable appeal. He could scarcely indeed have understood it, knowing as he did so little about the American mind. How such a delusion came to possess Mark Twain would be an interesting study in itself; but it was of the nature of our old democracy to believe that the feelings and opinions of the majority had a sort of divine sanction, the popular being regarded as *ipso facto* good. Under these conditions, a double standard of taste might well have seemed as natural to a man in Mark Twain's position as that other article of faith of the nineteenth century, the double standard of morals. Yet the "Connecticut Yankee" itself shows us how false the notion was. Mark Twain's plea was that he was "trying to uplift the mighty mass of the uncultivated." Actually, in this book, he debased them: he flattered their ignorance of history, he played on their

THE NOVELS OF UPTON SINCLAIR

prejudice against the old world, he drew their attention from the abuses of their own social life by focussing their indignation on the long-forgotten abuses of the Middle Ages, he confirmed them in their complacent belief that a shrewd Yankee mechanic possessed all the secrets of life that anyone ought to desire.

It is with a number of such instances in mind that I have read Mr. Upton Sinclair's three recent novels, "King Coal," "Jimmie Higgins" and "100%: the Story of a Patriot." Judged by the "cultivated-class standard," these books are as bad as books can be, weak, slovenly, deficient in all the qualities that make a work of art. Novels are novels; from the standpoint of criticism their subject-matter cannot save them. It is impossible to interest oneself in "winsome Irish lasses," in pretty stenographers whose "wicked little dimples lose no curtain calls," in "patriots" like Peter Gudge, in paragons like Jimmie Higgins—impossible because they do not exist in Mr. Sinclair's own imagination. They have no more existence than the villains and the heroes and the naughty ladies of the movies and the *Red Book Magazine*. Mr. Sinclair has no more respect for psychology than his mine-owners have for their employees; he has no more respect than Mr. Hearst for the intelligence of his readers. His novels are simply "reels."

I am speaking, as I say, from the "cultivated-class" standpoint. And now the question arises whether Mr. Sinclair is any better advised in his attempt to liberate the proletariat by this means than Mark Twain was in "trying to uplift the mighty mass of the uncultivated." In his advertisement of "100%" Mr. Sinclair quotes the opinion of one of his readers that he will have even more trouble than he had with "The Brass Check" in "getting the books printed fast enough." It is natural that Mr. Sinclair should be popular with the dispossessed: they who are so seldom flattered find in his pages a land of milk and honey. Here all the workers wear haloes of pure golden sunlight and all the capitalists have horns and tails; socialists with fashionable English wives invariably turn yellow at the appropriate moment, and rich men's sons are humbled in the dust, Irish lasses are always true and wives never understand their husbands, and all the good people are martyrs and all the patriots are vile. Mr. Sinclair says that the incidents in his books are based on fact and that his characters are studied from life. No doubt they are. But Mr. Sinclair, naturally enough, has seen what he wanted to see and studied what he wanted to study; and his special simplification of the social scene is one that inevitably makes glad the heart of the victim of our system. It fills this victim with emotion, the emotion of hatred and the emotion of self-pity. Mr. Sinclair's novels sell by the hundred thousand; the wonder is they do not sell by the million.

But suppose now that one wishes to see the dispossessed rise in their might and really, in the name of justice, take possession of the world. Suppose one wishes to see the class-system abolished, along with all the other unhappy things that Mr. Sinclair writes about. That is Mr. Sinclair's own desire; and he honestly believes that in writing as he does he contributes to this happy consummation. I cannot agree with him. In so far as Mr. Sinclair's books show us anything real they show us the utter helplessness, the benightedness, the naïveté of the American workers' movement. Jimmie Higgins does not exist as a character. He is a symbol, however, and one can read reality into him. He is the American worker incarnate. Well, was there ever a worker so little the master of his fate? That, in point of fact, is just the conclusion Mr. Sinclair wishes us to draw. But why is he so helpless? Because, for all his kindness and his courage, he is, from an intellectual and social point of view, unlike the English worker, the German, Italian, Russian, the merest infant; he knows nothing about life or human nature or economics or philosophy or even his enemies. How can he possibly set about advancing his own cause, how can he circumvent the wily patrioteers, how can he become anything but what he is, the mere football of everyone who knows more than he? Let us drop the "cultivated-class" standpoint and judge Mr. Sinclair's novels from the standpoint of the proletariat itself. They arouse the emotion of self-pity. Does that stimulate the worker or does it merely "console" him? They arouse the emotion of hatred. Does that teach him how to grapple with his oppressors or does it place him all the more at his oppressors' mercy? The most elementary knowledge of human nature tells us that there is only one answer to these questions.

The American workers' movement is weak: that we know. The workers' movements of Europe are, in comparison, strong: that we also know. But why are they strong? Because the masses of individuals that compose them are, relatively speaking, not intellectual and moral infants but instructed, well-developed, resourceful men. They waste little energy in "hating" their masters; they are too busy learning to understand them. They waste still less energy in pitying themselves; they are too busy establishing their rights. How much of this superior morale they owe to their superior education is a question not easily answered, but one thing is certain: nothing hinders the worker so much as books like Mr. Sinclair's. These false simplifications, these appeals to the martyr in human nature are so much dust thrown in the eyes of the proletariat. To the workers, themselves, in other words, Mr. Sinclair, with his cake and circuses, is more dangerous than all the business men he chastises with whips and scorpions.

To return, then, to the "cultivated-class standard," I respectfully urge that a book which is not good enough for me is not good enough for Mr. Sinclair's readers either. I further maintain that the only writers who can possibly aid in the liberation of humanity are those whose sole responsibility is to themselves as artists. Consider the best novels that have been written with a view to propaganda alone. Consider "Uncle Tom's Cabin." Mrs. Stowe undoubtedly helped to liberate the Negroes from slavery: but few today would deny that she "liberated" them from the frying-pan into the fire. She evoked the emotion of self-pity and the emotion of hatred, but she failed to make her readers think; and because of this the last state of the Negro is all but worse than the first. On the other hand, consider Turgenev who, in his "Sportsman's Sketches," wrote to please himself. He revealed the serf not as an Uncle Tom, a teary wax image, but as a man capable of pride, faith and thought; and the result was that the conscience of Russia has been occupied with nothing since but to rescue that thinking man and reinstate him in his rights. No writer can say how his work may serve the cause of liberty; but if he is sincere it cannot help serving this cause in the most unexpected ways. Thus, for example, Gorky in his autobiography describes how he got his first revolutionary feeling from Dumas, of all writers in the world. As a boy he used to pore over Dumas' romances, and it astonished him to hear of a society in which people were polite and considerate of one another. The streets of Paris became his Utopia, and it was then he began to dream of a day when his own Russia, the Russia of the disinherited, might also have its share of social grace and beauty. That was because Dumas, insincere as he was in other respects, conveyed a sincere picture of fine manners. "The persons," said Shelley (àpropos of literature, and expressing the whole truth), "the persons in whom this power takes its abode may often, as far as regards many portions of their nature, have little correspondence with the spirit of good of which it is the minister. But although they may deny and abjure, they are yet compelled to serve that which is seated on the throne of their own soul. And whatever systems they may have professed by support, they actually advance the interests of Liberty."

THE LITERARY LIFE IN AMERICA

THE LITERARY LIFE IN AMERICA

AMONG all the figures which, in Mrs. Wharton's "The Age of Innocence," make up the pallid little social foreground, the still more pallid middle distance, of the New York of forty years ago, there is none more pallid than the figure of Ned Winsett, the "man of letters untimely born in a world that had no need of letters." Winsett, we are told, "had published one volume of brief and exquisite literary appreciations," of which one hundred and twenty copies had been sold, and had then abandoned his calling and taken an obscure post on a women's weekly. "On the subject of *Hearth-fires* (as the paper was called) he was inexhaustibly entertaining," says Mrs. Wharton; "but beneath his fun lurked the sterile bitterness of the still young man who has tried and given up." Sterile bitterness, a bright futility, a beginning without a future: that is the story of Ned Winsett.

One feels, as one turns Mrs. Wharton's pages,

how symbolic this is of the literary life in America. I shall say nothing of the other arts, though the vital conditions of all the arts have surely much in common; I shall say nothing of America before the Civil War, for the America that New England dominated was a different nation from ours. But what immediately strikes one, as one surveys the history of our literature during the last half century, is the singular impotence of its creative spirit. That we have and have always had an abundance of talent is, I think, no less evident: what I mean is that so little of this talent succeeds in effectuating itself. Of how many of our modern writers can it be said that their work reveals a continuous growth, or indeed any growth, that they hold their ground tenaciously and preserve their sap from one decade to another? Where, to speak relatively, the characteristic evolution of the European writer is one of an ever-increasing differentiation, a progress towards the creation, the possession of a world absolutely his own (the world of Shaw, the world of Hardy, the world of Hamsun, of Gorky, of Anatole France), the American writer, having struck out with his new note, becomes—how often!—progressively less and less himself. The blighted career, the arrested career, the diverted career are, with us, the rule. The chronic state of our literature is that of a youthful promise which is never redeemed.

The great writer, the *grand écrivain,* has at the best of times appeared but once or twice in America: that is another matter. I am speaking, as I say, of the last half century, and I am speaking of the rank and file. There are those who will deny this characterization of our literature, pointing to what they consider the robust and wholesome corpus of our "normal" fiction. But this fiction, in its way, corroborates my point. What is the quality of the spirit behind it? How much does it contain of that creative element the character of which consists in dominating life instead of being dominated by it? Have these novelists of ours any world of their own as distinguished from the world they observe and reflect, the world they share with their neighbors? Is it a personal vision that informs them, or a mob-vision? The Danish writer, Johannes V. Jensen, has described their work as "journalism under exceptionally fortunate conditions." Journalism, on the whole, it assuredly is, and the chief of these fortunate conditions (fortunate for journalism!) has been the general failure of the writers in question to establish and develop themselves as individuals:

as they have rendered unto Caesar what was intended for God, is it any wonder that Caesar has waxed so fat? "The unfortunate thing," writes Mr. Montrose J. Moses, "is that the American drama" — but the observation is equally true of this fiction of ours—"has had many brilliant promises which have finally thinned out and never materialized." And again: "The American dramatist has always taken his logic second-hand; he has always allowed his theatrical sense to be a slave to managerial circumstance." The two statements are complementary, and they apply, as I say, to the whole of this "normal" literature. Managerial circumstance? Let us call it local patriotism, the spirit of the times, the hunger of the public for this, that or the other: to some one of these demands, these promptings from without, the "normal" American writer always allows himself to become a slave. It is the fact, indeed, of his being a slave to some demand from without that makes him "normal"—and something else than an artist.

The flourishing exterior of the main body of our contemporary literature, in short, represents anything but the integrity of an inner well-being. But even aside from this, one can count on one's two hands the American writers who are able to carry on the development and unfolding of their individualities, year in, year out, as every competent man of affairs carries on his business. What fate overtakes the rest? Shall I begin to run over some of those names, familiar to us all, names that have signified so much promise and are lost in what Gautier calls "the limbo where moan (in the company of babes) still-born vocations, abortive attempts, larvæ of ideas that have won neither wings nor shapes"? Shall I mention the writers—but they are countless!—who have lapsed into silence or involved themselves in barren eccentricities, or who have been turned into machines? The poets who, at the outset of their careers, find themselves extinguished like so many candles? The novelists who have been unable to grow up, and remain withered boys of seventeen? The critics who find themselves overtaken in mid-career by a hardening of the spiritual arteries? Our writers all but universally lack the power of growth, the endurance that enables one to continue to produce personal work after the freshness of youth has gone.

Such is the aspect of our contemporary literature; beside that of almost any European country, it is indeed one long list of spiritual casualties. For it is not that the talent is wanting, but that somehow this talent fails to fulfil itself.

This being so, how much one would like to assume, with certain of our critics, that the American writer is a sort of Samson bound with the brass fetters of the Philistines and requiring only to have those fetters cast off in order to be able to conquer the world! That, as I understand it, is the position of Mr. Dreiser, who recently remarked of certain of our novelists: "They succeeded in writing but one book before the iron hand of convention took hold of them." There is this to be said for the argument, that if the American writer as a type shows less resistance than the European writer it is plainly because he has been insufficiently equipped, stimulated, nourished by the society into which he has been born. In this sense the American environment is answerable for the literature it has produced. But what is significant is that the American writer *does* show less resistance; and as literature is nothing but the expression of power, of the creative will, of "free will," in short, is it not more accurate to say, not that the "iron hand of convention" takes hold of our writers, but that our writers yield to the "iron hand of convention"? Samson had lost his virility before the Philistines bound him; it was because he had

THE LITERARY LIFE IN AMERICA

lost his virility that the Philistines were able to bind him. The American writer who "goes wrong" is in a similar case. "I have read," says Mr. Dreiser, of Jack London, "several short stories which proved what he could do. But he did not feel that he cared for want and public indifference. Hence his many excellent romances." *He did not feel that he cared for want and public indifference.* Even Mr. Dreiser, as we observe, determinist that he is, admits a margin of free will, for he represents Jack London as having made a choice. What concerns us now, however, is not a theoretical but a practical question, the fact, namely, that the American writer as a rule is actuated not by faith but by fear, that he cannot meet the obstacles of "want and public indifference" as the European writer meets them, that he is, indeed, and as if by nature, a journeyman and a hireling.

As we see, then, the creative will in this country is a weak and sickly plant. Of the innumerable talents that are always emerging about us there are few that come to any sort of fruition. The rest wither early; they are transformed into those neuroses that flourish on our soil as orchids flourish in the green jungle. The sense of this failure is written all over our literature. Do we not know what depths of disappointment underlay the cynicism of Mark Twain and Henry Adams and Ambrose Bierce? Have we failed to recognize, in the surly contempt with which the author of "The Story of a Country Town" habitually speaks of writers and writing, the unconscious cry of sour grapes of a man whose creative life was arrested in youth? Are we unaware of the bitterness with which, in certain letters of his later years, Jack London regretted the miscarriage of his gift? There is no denying that for half a century the American writer as a type has gone down to defeat.

Now why is this so? Why does the American writer, relatively speaking, show less resistance than the European writer? Plainly, as I have just said, because he has been insufficiently equipped, stimulated, nourished by the society into which he has been born. If our creative spirits are unable to grow and mature, it is a sign that there is something wanting in the soil from which they spring and the conditions that surround them. Is it not, for that matter, a sign of some more general failure in our life?

"At the present moment," wrote Mr. Chesterton in one of his early essays ("The Fallacy of the Young Nation"), struck by the strange anæmia of so many American artists, "at the present moment the matter which America has very seriously to consider is not how near it is to its birth and beginning, but how near it may be to its end. . . . The English colonies have produced no great artists, and that fact may prove that they are still full of silent possibilities and reserve force. But America has produced great artists and that fact most certainly means that she is full of a fine futility and the end of all things. Whatever the American men of genius are, they are not young gods making a young world. Is the art of Whistler a brave, barbaric art, happy and headlong? Does Mr. Henry James infect us with the spirit of a school-boy? No, the colonies have not spoken, and they are safe. Their silence may be the silence of the unborn. But out of America has come a sweet and startling cry, as unmistakable as the cry of a dying man." That there is some truth behind this, that the soil of our society is arid and impoverished, is indicated by the testimony of our own poets. One has only to consider what George Cabot Lodge wrote in 1904 in one of his letters: "We are a dying race, as every race must be of which the men are, as men and not accumulators, third-rate"; one has only to consider the writings of Messrs. Frost, Robinson, and Masters, in whose presentation of our life, in the West as well as in the East, the individual as a spiritual unit invariably suffers defeat. Fifty years ago, J. A. Froude, on a visit to this country, wrote to one of his friends: "From what I see of the Eastern states I do not anticipate any very great things as likely to come out of the Americans. . . . They are generous with their money, they have tenderness and quiet good humor; but the Anglo-Saxon power is running to seed and I don't think will revive." When we consider the colorlessness and insipidity of our latter-day life (faithfully reflected in the novels of Howells and his successors), the absence from it of profound passions and intense convictions, of any representative individuals who can be compared in spiritual force with Emerson, Thoreau and so many of their contemporaries, its uniformity and its uniform tepidity, then the familiar saying, "Our age has been an age of management, not of ideas or of men," assumes indeed a very sinister import. I go back to the poet Lodge's letters. "Was there ever," he writes, "such an anomaly as the American man? In practical affairs his cynicism, energy and capacity are simply stupefying, and in every other respect he is a sentimental idiot possessing neither the interest, the capacity nor the desire for even the most elementary processes of independent thought. . . . His wife finds him so sexually inapt that she refuses to bear him children and so drivelling in every way except as a money-getter that she compels him to expend his energies solely in that direction while she leads a discontented, sterile, stunted life. . . ." Is this to be denied? And does it not in part explain that lovelessness of the American scene which has bred the note of a universal resentment in so much of our contemporary fiction? As well expect figs from thistles as men from such a soil who are robust enough to prefer spiritual to material victories and who are capable of achieving them.

It is unnecessary to go back to Taine in order to realize that here we have a matrix as unpropitious as possible for literature and art. If our writers wither early, if they are too generally pliant, passive, acquiescent, anæmic, how much is this not due to the heritage of pioneering, with its burden of isolation, nervous strain, excessive work and all the racial habits that these have engendered?

Certainly, for example, if there is anything that counts in the formation of the creative spirit it is that long infancy to which John Fiske, rightly or wrongly, attributed the emergence of man from the lower species. In the childhood of almost every great writer one finds this protracted incubation, this slow stretch of years in which the unresisting organism opens itself to the influences of life. It was so with Hawthorne, it was so with Whitman in the pastoral America of a century ago: they were able to mature, these brooding spirits, because they had given themselves for so long to life before they began to react upon it. That is the old-world childhood still, in a measure; how different it is from the modern American childhood may be seen if one compares, for example, the first book ("Boyhood") of "Pelle the Conqueror" with any of those innumerable tales in which our novelists show us that in order to succeed in life one cannot be up and doing too soon. The whole temper of our society, if one is to judge from these documents, is to hustle the American out of his childhood, teaching him at no age at all how to repel life and get the best of it and build up the defences behind which he is going to fight for his place in the sun. Who can deny that this racial habit succeeds in its unconscious aim—to produce sharp-witted men of business? But could anything be deadlier to the poet, the artist, the writer?

Everything in such an environment, it goes without saying, tends to repress the creative and to stimulate the competitive impulses. A certain Irish poet has observed that all he ever learned of poetry he got from talking with peasants along the road. Whitman might have said almost as much, even of New York, the New York of seventy years ago. But what nourishment do they offer receptive spirits today, the harassed, inhibited mob of our fellow-countrymen, eaten up with the "itch of ill-advised activity"—what encouragement to become anything but automata like themselves? And what direction, in such a society, does the instinct of emulation receive, that powerful instinct of adolescence? A certain visitor of Whitman's has described him as living in a house "as cheerless as an ash-barrel," a house indeed "like that in which a very destitute mechanic" might have lived. Is it not symbolic, that picture, of the esteem in which our democracy holds the poet? If today the man of many dollars is no longer the hero of the editorial page and the baccalaureate address, still, or rather more than ever, it is the "aggressive" type that overshadows every corner of our civilization; the intellectual man who has gone his own way was never less the hero. Many, in short, are the elements in our society that contribute to form a selection constantly working against the survival of the creative type.

It is certainly true that none of these unfavorable conditions could have had such a baleful effect upon our literature if there had been others to counteract them. An aristocratic tradition, if we had ever had it, would have kept open among us the right of way of the free individual, would have preserved the claims of mere living. "It is curious to observe," writes Nietzsche in one of his letters, "how anyone who soon leaves the traditional highway in order to travel on his own proper path always has more or less the sense of being an exile, a condemned criminal, a fugitive from mankind." If that is true in the old world, where society is so much more complex and offers the individual so much more latitude, how few could ever have had the strength in a society like ours, which has always placed such a premium on conformity, to become and remain themselves? Is it fanciful indeed to see in the famous "remorse" of Poe the traces left by this dereliction of the tribal law on the unconscious mind of an artist of unique force and courage? Similarly, a tradition of voluntary poverty would have provided us with an escape from the importunities of bourgeois custom. But aside from the fact that even so simple a principle as this depends largely for its life on precedent (Whitman and the painter

THE LITERARY LIFE IN AMERICA

Ryder are almost alone among latter-day Americans in having discovered it for themselves), aside from the fact that to secede from the bourgeois system is, in America, to subject oneself to quite peculiar penalties (did it ever occur to Mark Twain that he *could* be honorably poor?)—aside from all this, poverty in the new world is not the same thing as poverty in the old: one has only to think of Charles Lamb and all the riches that London freely gave him, all the public resources he had at his disposal, to appreciate the difference. With us poverty means in the end an almost inevitable intellectual starvation. Consider such a plaint as Sidney Lanier's: "I could never describe to you" (he writes to Bayard Taylor) "what a mere drought and famine my life has been, as regards that multitude of matters which I fancy one absorbs when one is in an atmosphere of art, or when one is in conversational relationship with men of letters, with travellers, with persons who have either seen, or written, or done large things. Perhaps you know that, with us of the younger generation in the South since the war, pretty much the whole of life has been merely not dying." That is what poverty means in America, poverty and isolation, for Lanier, whose talent, as we can see today, was hopelessly crippled by it, was mistaken if he supposed that there was anything peculiar to the South in that plight of his: it has been the plight of the sensitive man everywhere in America and at all times. Add to poverty the want of a society devoted to intellectual things and we have such a fate as Herman Melville's in New York. "What he lacked," says Mr. Frank Jewett Mather, "was possibly only health and nerve, but perhaps, even more, companionship of a friendly, critical, understanding sort. In London, where he must have been hounded out of his corner, I can imagine Melville carrying the reflective vein to literary completion." Samuel Butler was not entirely mistaken when he jotted down the following observation in his notebook: "America will have her geniuses, as every other country has, in fact she has already had one in Walt Whitman, but I do not think America is a good place in which to be a genius. A genius can never expect to have a good time anywhere, if he is a genuine article, but America is about the last place in which life will be endurable at all for an inspired writer of any kind."

To such circumstances as these, I say, the weakness of our literary life is due. But the lack of great leaders, of a strong and self-respecting literary guild (the one results from the other) —is not this our chief misfortune? In the best of circumstances, and considering all the devils that beset the creative spirit, a strong impulse is scarcely enough to carry the writer through: he must feel not only that he is doing what he wishes to do but that what he is doing *matters.* If dozens of American writers have fallen by the wayside because they have met with insuperable obstacles, dozens of others have fallen, with all their gifts, because they have lost interest in their work, because they have ceased to "see the necessity" of it. This is just the point where the presence of a leader, of a local tradition, a school, a guild, makes all the difference. "With the masters I converse," writes Gauguin in his journal. "Their example fortifies me. When I am tempted to falter I blush before them." If that could have been true of Gauguin, the "Wolf," who walked by himself as few have walked, what shall we say of other men whose artistic integrity, whose faith in themselves, is exposed every day to the corroding influences of a mechanized civilization? It would be all very well if literature were merely a mode of "having a good time": I am speaking of those, the real artists, who, with Nietzsche, make a distinction (illusory perhaps) between "happiness" and "work," and I say that these men have always fed on the thought of greatness and on the propinquity of greatness. It was not for nothing that Turgenev bore in his memory, as a talisman, the image of Pushkin; that Gorky, having seen Tolstoy once, sitting among the boulders on the seashore, felt everything in him blending in one happy thought, "I am not an orphan on the earth, so long as this man lives on it." The presence of such men immeasurably raises the morale of the literary life: that is what Chekov meant when he said, "I am afraid of Tolstoy's death," and is it not true that the whole contemporary literature of England has drawn virtue from Thomas Hardy? The sense that one is *working in a great line:* this, more than anything else perhaps, renews one's confidence in the "quaint mania of passing one's life wearing oneself out over words," as Flaubert called it, in the still greater folly of pursuing one's ego when everything in life combines to punish one for doing so. The successful pursuit of the ego is what makes literature; this requires not only a certain inner intensity but also a certain courage, and it is doubtful whether, in any nation, any considerable number of men can summon up that courage and maintain it unless they have *seen the thing done.*

THE LITERARY LIFE IN AMERICA

The very notion that such a life is either possible or desirable, the notion that such a life exists even, can hardly occur to the rank and file: some individual has to start the ball rolling, some individual of extraordinary force and audacity, and where is that individual to be found in our modern American literature? Whitman is the unique instance, for Henry James was an exile; and Whitman was not only essentially of an earlier generation, he was an invalid who folded his hands in mid-career.

Of those others what can we say, those others whose gifts have fitted them to be our leaders? Howells once observed of the American drama that "mainly it has been gay as our prevalent mood is, mainly it has been honest, as our habit is, in cases where we believe we can afford it." In this gently ironical pleasantry one seems to discern the spirit of the literature of the age preceding ours. But it was Howells himself who, in order to arrive at the doctrine that "the more smiling aspects of life are the more American," deliberately, as he has told us, and professed realist that he was, averted his eyes from the darker side of life. And Mark Twain suppressed his real beliefs about man and the universe. And Henry Adams refused to sponsor in public the novels that revealed what he considered to be the truth about American society. At its very headwaters, as we see, this modern literature of ours has failed to flow clear: the creative impulse in these men, richly endowed as they were, was checked and compromised by too many other impulses, social and commercial. If one is to blame anything for this, it is the immense insecurity of our life, which is due to its chaotic nature; for one is not entitled to expect greatness even of those who have the greatest gifts, and of these men Adams was alone secure; of Howells and Mark Twain, frontiersmen as they were, it may be said that they were obliged to compromise, consciously or unconsciously, to gain a foothold in the one corner of the country where men were able to exist as writers at all. But if these men were unable to establish their independence (and one has only to recall the notorious Gorky dinner in order to perceive the ignominy of their position), what can one expect of the rank and file? Great men form a sort of wind-shield behind which the rest of their profession are able to build up their own defences; they establish a right of way for the others; they command a respect for their profession, they arouse in the public a concern for it, an interest in it, from which the others benefit. As things are, the

THE LITERARY LIFE IN AMERICA

literary guild in America is not greatly respected, nor does it too greatly respect itself. In "My Literary Passions," Howells, after saying that his early reading gave him no standing among other boys, observes: "I have since found that literature gives one no more certain station in the world of men's activities, either idle or useful. We literary folk try to believe that it does, but that is all nonsense. At every period of life among boys or men we are accepted when they are at leisure and want to be amused, and at best we are tolerated rather than accepted." That is ironical too, but a little pathetic as well. Imagine Gorky or Hamsun or Bernard Shaw "trying to believe" that literature gives him a certain station in the world of men's activities! Howells, conscientious craftsman that he was, instinctively shared, in regard to the significance of his vocation, the feeling of our pragmatic philosophers, who justify the intellectual life by showing how useful it is—not to mention Mr. R. W. Chambers, who has remarked that writers "are not held in excessive esteem by really busy people, the general idea being—which is usually true—that literature is a godsend to those unfitted for real work." After this one can easily understand why it is that our novelists take such pains to be mistaken for business men.

So much for the conditions, or at least a few of them, that have prevented our literature from getting its head above water. If America is littered with extinct talents, the halt, the maimed and the blind, it is for reasons with which we are all too familiar; and those to whom the creative life is the principle of human movement look on this wreckage of everything that is most precious to society and ask themselves what our fathers meant when they extolled the progress of our civilization. But let us look facts in the face. Mr. Sinclair Lewis says that we are in the midst of a revival and that we are too humble in supposing that our contemporary literature is inferior to that of England. That we are in the midst of a revival no one doubts, but it is the sustained career that makes a literature; without the evidence of this we can hope much but we can affirm nothing. And what we can see is that, with all its hope, the morale of the literary profession in this country is just what its antecedents have made it. I am reminded of the observation of a friend who has reason to know, that the Catholic Church in America, great as it is in numbers and organization, still depends on the old world for its models, its taskmasters and its inspiration; for the American priest, as a rule, does not feel the vocation as

THE LITERARY LIFE IN AMERICA

the European feels it. I am reminded of the American labor movement which, prosperous as it is in comparsion with the labor movements of Europe, is unparalleled for the feebleness of its representatives. I am reminded of certain brief experiences in the American university world which have led me to believe that the professors who radiate a genuine light and warmth are far more likely to be Russians, Germans, Englishmen, Dutchmen, and Swedes than the children of '76. The hostility of the pioneers to the special career still operates to prevent in the American mind the powerful, concentrated pursuit of any non-utilitarian way of life. Considered with reference to its higher manifestations, life itself has been thus far, in modern America, a failure. Of this the failure of our literature is merely emblematic.

Mr. Mencken, who shares this belief, urges that the only hope of a change for the better lies in the development of a native aristocracy that will stand between the writer and the public, supporting him, appreciating him, forming as it were a *cordon sanitaire* between the individual and the mob. That no change can come without the development of an aristocracy of some sort, some nucleus of the more gifted, energetic and determined, one can hardly doubt.

But how can one expect the emergence of an aristocracy outside the creative class, and devoted to its welfare, unless and until the creative class itself reveals the sort of will that attracts its ministrations? "The notion that a people can run itself and its affairs anonymously is now well known to be the silliest of absurdities." Thus William James, in defence of the aristocratic principle; and what he says is as applicable to literature as to every other department of social life. But he continues: "Mankind does nothing save through initiatives on the part of inventors, great and small, and imitation by the rest of us—these are the sole factors alive in human progress. Individuals of genius show the way, and set the pattern, which common people then adopt and follow." In other words, so far as literature is concerned, the burden of proof lies on the writer himself—which brings one back to a truism: it is not for the public or any aristocratic minority within the public to understand the writer, it is for the writer to create the taste by which he is understood. Is it not by this indeed (in a measure, at least) that we recognize the creator?

Certainly if our contemporary literature is not respected, if it has not been able to rally to its support the sensitive public that already exists in this country, it is partly because this literature has not respected itself. That there has been every reason for this makes no difference; that it has begun to respect itself again makes no difference either, for when a people has lost confidence in its literature, and has had grounds for losing confidence, one cannot be surprised if it insists a little cynically upon being "shown." The public supported Mark Twain and Howells and the men of their generation, it admired them for what was admirable in them, but it was aware, if only unconsciously, that there was a difference between them and the men of the generation before them; and in consequence of this the whole stock of American literature fell. But those who insist in our day that America prefers European writers to its own because America is still a colony of Europe cannot ignore the significant fact that at a time when America was still more truly colonial American writers had all the prestige in this country that European writers have at present; and it is not entirely because at that time the country was more homogeneous. Poe and Thoreau found little support in the generation I speak of, as Whitman found little support in the generation that followed it. On the other hand, there were no European writers (and it was an age of great writers in Europe) who were held in higher esteem in this country than Hawthorne, Emerson, Motley and one or two others almost equally distinguished, as well from a European as from an American point of view; there were few, if any, European writers, in fact, who were esteemed in this country as highly as they. How can one explain it? How can one explain why, at a time when America, in every other department of life, was more distinctly colonial than it is now, American literature commanded the full respect of Americans, while today, when the colonial tradition is vanishing all about us, it so little commands their respect that they go after any strange god from England? The problem is far from simple, but among its many explanations one can hardly deny that there were in that period a number of writers of unusual power, who made the most of their power and followed their artistic conscience and who by this fact built up a public confidence in themselves and the literature they represented. Does it matter at all whether we today enjoy these writers or not? They were men of spiritual force, three or four of them: that is the important point. If the emerging writers of our epoch find themselves handicapped by the scepticism of the public, they have only to remember that they are themselves for the most part in the formative stage and that they have to live down the recent past of their profession.

Meanwhile, what constitutes a literature is the spiritual force of the individuals who compose it. If our literature is to grow it can only be through the development of a sense of "free will" on the part of our writers themselves. To be, to feel oneself, a "victim" is in itself not to be an artist, for it is the nature of the artist to live, not in the world of which he is an effect, but in the world of which he is the cause, the world of his own creation. For this reason, the pessimistic determinism of the present age is, from the point of view of literature, of a piece with the optimistic determinism of the age that is passing. What this pessimistic determinism reveals, however, is a *consciousness of the situation:* to that extent it represents a gain, and one may even say that to be conscious of the situation is half the battle. If we owed nothing else to Mr. Dreiser, we should owe him enough for the tragic sense of the waste of American life which his books communicate. It remains true that if we resent this life it is only a sign of our weakness, of the harm we have permitted this civilization to do us, of our imperfectly realized freedom; for to the creative spirit in its free state the external world is merely an impersonal point of departure. Thus it is certain that as long as the American writer shares what James Bryce called the "mass fatalism" of the American people, our literature will remain the sterile, inferior phenomenon which, on the whole, it is.

"What we want," wrote Henry Adams in 1862 to his brother Charles, "is a *school*. We want a national set of young men like ourselves or better, to start new influences not only in politics, but in literature, in law, in society, and throughout the whole social organism of the country—a national school of our own generation. And that is what America has no power to create. . . . It's all random, insulated work, for special and temporary and personal purposes. And we have no means, power or hope of combined action for any unselfish end." *That is what America has no power to create.* But can it be said that any nation has ever created a school? Here we have the perfect illustration of that mass fatalism of which I have spoken, and Henry Adams himself, in his passivity, is the type of it. Secure as he was, uniquely secure, why did he refuse to accept the responsibility of those novels in which he expressed the contempt of a powerful and cultivated mind for the meanness of the guiding element in American society? In the darkest and most chaotic hours of our spiritual history the individual has possessed a measure of free will only to renounce it: if Henry Adams had merely signed his work he might by that very fact have become the founder of the school that he desired. But it is true that in that generation the impulses of youth were, with extraordinary unanimity, focussed upon a single end, the exploitation of the continent; the material opportunities that American life offered were too great and too all-engrossing, and it is unlikely that any considerable minority could have been rallied for any non-utilitarian cause. Sixty years later this school remains the one thing necessary: the reforestation of our spiritual territory depends upon it. And in more than one sense the times are favorable. The closing of the frontier seems to promise for this country an intenser life than it has known before; a large element of the younger generation, estranged from the present order, exists in a state of ferment that renders it highly susceptible to new ideas; the country swarms with half-artists who have ceased to conform to the law of the tribe but have not accepted the discipline of their own individual spirits. "What I chiefly desire for you," wrote

Ibsen to Brandes at the outset of his career, "is a genuine, full-blooded egoism, which shall force you for a time to regard what concerns you yourself as the only thing of any consequence, and everything else as non-existent. . . . There is no way in which you can benefit society more than by coining the metal you have in yourself." The second half of this rather blunt counsel of perfection is implied in the first, and it connotes a world of things merely to name which would be to throw into relief the infantility of the American writer as a type. By what prodigies of alert self-adaptation, of discrimination self-scrutiny, of conscious effort, does the creative will come into its own! As for ourselves, weak as too many of us are, ignorant, isolated, all too easily satisfied, and scarcely as yet immune from the solicitations of the mob, we still have this advantage, that an age of reaction is an age that stirs the few into a consciousness of themselves.